W9-DJH-021

Black/Brown/White Relations

Black/Brown/White Relations

Relations

Race Relations in the 1970s

Edited by
Charles V. Willie

Transaction Books
New Brunswick, N.J.

Copyright © 1977 by Transaction, Inc.,
New Brunswick, New Jersey 08903

All rights reserved under International and Pan-American Copyright Conventions. No part of this book may be reproduced or transmitted in any form or by any means, electronic or mechanical, including photocopy, recording, or any information storage and retrieval system, without prior permission in writing from the publisher. All inquiries should be addressed to Transaction Books, Rutgers University, New Brunswick, New Jersey 08903.

Library of Congress Catalog Number: 76-1770.
ISBN: 0-87855-102-6 (cloth); 0-87855-596-X (paper).
Printed in the United States of America.

Library of Congress Cataloging in Publication Data

Main entry under title:

Black/brown/white relations.

    Includes index.
    1.   United States–Race question–Addresses,
essays, lectures, etc.   2.   Race discrimination–
United States–Addresses, essays, lectures.
3.   United States–Social conditions–1960-
–Addresses, essays, lectures.   I.   Willie, Charles
Vert, 1927-
E184.A1B553   301.45'1'0973   76-1770

ISBN 0-87855-102-6
ISBN 0-87855-596-X pbk.

Robert Manning Strozier Library

JUN 29 197t

Tallahassee, Florida

This book is dedicated
with joy and thanksgiving
to
John and Helen Hines

Contents

Preface

The state of race relations research is probably best described by W. Curtis Banks, a psychologist. "I think we have worn out simple notions of attitudes, stereotypes, and scapegoating long ago," he states, "in attempting to both explain and predict interracial behavior." Further, he talks about "the exhaustion of old approaches and the absence of provocative new ones."

The focus on race, power, and social change in this book is not so much a new approach as it is a new emphasis. [The attitudes and beliefs of people are influenced greatly by the groups and institutions in which they participate. The successful containment of racial prejudice and discrimination in society will result not only from change in the biased attitudes of individuals but also from change in the racist regulations of institutions. This book emphasizes the institutional source and support of racism and prejudice, and suggests ways of modifying social systems. Particular attention is called to the need to use a flexible methodology that can change in accordance with the requirements of each situation.]

The authors also deal with definitions of the problem of race relations in the 1970s in the United States and with strategies for institutional change. Seven chapters are original and are published for the first time in this collection. They are chapters by: Jewelle Taylor Gibbs; David Owens; Curtis Banks, Janet Hubbard, and Joseph

9

Vannoy; Ann H. Beuf; Nijole Benokraitis and Joe Feagin; and the editor. Most of the remaining chapters were first published in *transaction/Society* magazine.

The authors are black, brown, and white, male and female, young and older, and identify with many different fields, including literature, sociology, social work, education, political science, and other behavioral and social sciences. Their diversity is something of value in providing perspectives on the complex structure and process of race relations in America.

The editor is grateful to the authors for permitting their excellent work to be published in this book and to the publisher of *transaction/Society* magazine for permission to reprint several articles. Acknowledged with appreciation also is the helpful editorial advice given by Mary E. Curtis and Dorothy Judd Sickels and the fine clerical work performed by Mary Walsh, who typed part of the manuscript.

The editor is thankful for the loving kindness expressed by members of his family during the preparation of this book. Mary Sue, Sarah Susannah, Martin Charles, and James Theodore are his major sources of support. They make race relations a living and loving reality.

Introduction

Race, Power, and Social Change

During an era of separatism, estrangement, polarization, and deep social cleavage, the source of knowledge one is willing to trust can be a serious impediment to knowing. With reference to books, we have used all kinds of rationalizations of why one book is better than another in dealing with a particular topic. Seldom do we grapple with the fundamental question: which writer are we willing to trust? This is a real issue in the sociology of knowledge, especially with reference to race relations.

Since the Civil War, America has been struggling with the issue of race relations and supposedly seeking an answer. One reason the answer of racial reconciliation has eluded us is that we have been unwilling to hear and believe any researchers, reporters, or analysts except the ones with whom we identify. What is it like to be black in America? This is a question that has troubled whites for many years. But whites tend to doubt reports on the black experience unless they are prepared by whites.

J. Saunders Redding, a black intellectual, gifted writer, member of the Phi Beta Kappa editorial board of *The American Scholar,* and a college professor, wrote a most revealing book entitled *On Being Negro in America* (10). His book never received the attention it deserved. Apparently whites were unwilling to trust a black to truthfully explain his circumstances of life. But *Black Like Me* was written by John Griffin, a gifted white writer who is committed to the cause of justice (3). He experimented with a number of chemicals until he was able to darken his skin without any permanent side effects. Then he traveled throughout the Southland as if he were black. The book describes his experiences and is on the social-studies reading lists of high schools throughout the country. There probably are many reasons why Griffin's book about blacks is more widely read than Redding's book. One of these reasons is best explained by a principle in the sociology of knowledge stated by Michael Polanyi— that "each person can know directly very little of truth and must trust others for the rest" (6, p. 10). In America, whites tend to be more trusting of other whites than they are of blacks to advance their knowledge on what it is like to be black.

The Carnegie Corporation cast about for a scholar to do a thorough-going study of "the Negro in the United States" several decades ago. Gunnar Myrdal, a Swedish economist, was retained. Myrdal, of course, was white. He published An American Dilemma, a book that was widely read and has been reissued (7). The scholarly works of E. Franklin Frazier, a black sociologist, on The Negro Family (1) and The Negro in the United States (2) never received the wide readership that An American Dilemma received. Robert Merton has stated that Myrdal was retained because he was an "outsider." Merton, of course, was using the nation-state as a frame of reference (6, p. 35). But using race as a frame of reference, I claim that Myrdal was retained to do a study of blacks in the United States because he was an "insider," which is to say he was white. Whites could believe a thorough-going study about blacks only if it was conducted by one who was white.

Our study of black students at white colleges reveals a similar trend among blacks. On the basis of student responses, we concluded that "blacks must accept the person before they can accept his or her ideas" (13, p. 50). There are widespread complaints among college students that "black authors and black poets are ignored. Because black literature is seldom assigned, black students. . .[say] that [they] don't learn much that would add to their abilities" (13, p. 45). In his discussion of insiders and outsiders, Merton explains this reaction on the part of blacks as a predictable outcome. He states that, "When a nation, race, ethnic group, or any other powerful collectivity has long extolled its own admirable qualities and expressly or by implication, deprecated the qualities of others, it invites and provides the potential for counterethnocentrism" (6, p. 18). In their counterethnocentrism, blacks also tend to project their own conception of what it is like to be white in America and these projections sometimes are a distortion of the white experience.

There is a self-centeredness among groups that causes their members to be interested in others only in relation to themselves. For example, we have prepared research reports on the black family and social class. We tried to examine the way of life of blacks on their own merits and not as deviant forms of behavior from some white "ideal types." One reviewer liked the material, thought it had promise, but suggested some changes. A suggested alteration was that there ought to be an elaboration on the implications of the sociology of black family life for whites. The interests of this reviewer, who was white, were quite similar to the interests of a black student at an integrated college who was demanding more courses that are relevant. When pressed for a definition of relevancy, he replied "relevancy is anything about me." This student and the reviewer indicate that self-centeredness is not the exclusive property of any racial group. But when the publishers are white and the market for publications is predominantly white, self-centeredness has a great deal to do with what gets published and, therefore, must be considered an important component in the sociology of knowledge pertaining to our understanding of race relations, particularly if published material is used as the chief source of knowledge.

With reference to family life, I have the distinct impression that many white scholars, for example, Daniel Patrick Moynihan, are more interested in studying and writing about the weaknesses in the black family and factors associated with its breakdown (11). Many black scholars, for example, Robert Hill, are more interested in studying the strengths in the black family and factors associated with its stability (4). An adequate sociology of black family life requires studies of strengths and weaknesses. The words and works of authors of both orientations should be published and studied.

I draw the reader's attention to Max Weber's idea that "problems investigated, and hence the concepts useful for their solution, [are] inevitably relative to the particular values involved in the situation and to the scientific interests of the observer" (8, p. 292). Because I agree with Weber, I believe that it is necessary and essential to include here authors of different races, sexes, and ages, so that their different perspectives derived from their "different social locations" can serve as a built-in self-corrective within the book. I believe the authors have fulfilled this goal. For example, Edward Greer gives a detailed analysis of how blacks may seize power through the political process. He uses Gary, Indiana, as an illustration. The mayor of

Atlanta, Georgia, has said that the 1970s have ushered in a new era of black achievement "perhaps most striking of all in the field of politics." He said, "we see black elected officials on every level of government—local, state, and national—giving voice to the hopes and aspirations of the masses of people who for so long were denied a part in their government" (5, p. 6). But Lee Sloan and Robert French present material in this book that mutes such optimism. They indicate that part of the push for metropolitan government in Jacksonville, Florida—which was campaigned for under the banner of "good government reform"—was an attempt on the part of whites to remain in control. As more whites left the city, and as the number of blacks increased, the "good government" interests proposed that the city of Jacksonville and Duval County should consolidate. This experience indicates that whites probably will not hand over local political control to blacks without a struggle, which probably will involve the use of legitimate rather than illegal means. The Gary and Jacksonville chapters in this book indicate how this struggle is likely to be waged. These reports indicate that there is a factual basis for both optimism and pessimism with respect to the use of government as a means of resisting or facilitating the sharing of power. This kind of information is made available because authors are included who identify with different groups and who, therefore, have different perspectives on race relations.

In the past, most investigations of race relations focused upon the attitudes of individuals. We now know that there may be a divergence between private attitudes and public actions. For example, in our study of black and white students at predominantly white colleges, we found that only ten percent of the white males believed that blacks should date blacks only. Yet the actions of these white males were quite different from their attitudes: "The closest friends for 71 percent of the white men in our study are white, and 64 percent say that they have limited their dating to whites" (12, p. 76). Black men also exhibit incongruence between attitudes and actions: "one-fourth of [the black] men said that blacks should have separate housing on campus." Of the separatists in attitude about living arrangements, about half were integrationists in their dating practices (12, p. 78). Attitudes and actions are not always the same.

With reference to racial prejudice, Thomas Pettigrew has estimated that about "three-fifths of white Americans may well be conforming bigots." This means that their attitudes are more flexible than once believed and are responsive to the social context and its pressures (9, pp. 290-91). In the light of this finding, Pettigrew believes a model for remedial action should place the "greatest importance as a target for change not on individual prejudice itself but on the racist institutional structures that shape and support the bigotry of individuals" (9, pp. 293-94).

This book resists the temptation to dwell upon the attitudes of individuals. Already there is a fairly large body of knowledge about prejudice. I have given more attention to discriminatory actions that have been institutionalized by government and voluntary associations. Especially considered are those actions which enhance, liberate, or restrict the behavior of individuals in one racial group compared with the behavior of individuals in another.

Moreover, I have examined the multiple responses that individuals of the same group may make to the same situation. Aggression, for example, is not the only action that one should anticipate as a reaction to the frustration of racial oppression. Withdrawal and cooperation are possible reactions, too. It is important to recognize the variety of actions and reactions and to examine the conditions under which one or another is likely to occur, and also the consequences of different actions and reactions for the dominant and subdominant individuals and the society at-large.

When this approach is followed, the study of race relations in the United States is lifted from concern largely with attitudes and interpersonal associations to concern about social norms, organizational sanctions, institutional regulations, and culture values. These support and sustain individuals and can influence their behavior. Moreover, our social practices that restrict the opportunities available to the members of one race compared with another often are initiated without a racist goal in mind. Pettigrew illustrates this by referring to the Harvard tradition of requiring the publication of scholarly works as one criterion for being selected for the tenured faculty. He said that "the aim was praiseworthy—namely, to ensure a faculty of high quality. Yet the publishing requirement effectively acted to restrict the recruitment of black professors, for most of them carried heavy teaching loads in predominantly black colleges, which limited their time to write. Not surprisingly, then, Harvard University in the 1960s found itself with only a handful of black faculty members. . . . This example can be repeated almost endlessly in American society," he said. Pettigrew is aware of the fact that this institutional requirement had a positive function, but he believes that it is possible to replace such arrangements as these with others "that serve the same positive functions equally well without the racist consequences" (9, pp. 275-76). This book is dedicated to providing some of the information necessary for achieving this goal.

The approach is realistic, however, and identifies the relationships among the races in America as a struggle for power. Thus, less attention is given to the immorality of racial oppression. More concern is focused on the structure and process of social organization and change, institutional arrangements, and methods of balancing and redistributing power in the community. A moral and ethical society is something of value and I believe that a just society has a higher probability of surviving than an unjust society. However, I have given more consideration to social arrangements rather than individual adaptations because the former sustain the latter and encourage persons to continue to hold prejudiced or unprejudiced attitudes, since most bigotry in America is of the conforming variety.

Moreover, I shall show that when power is concentrated, countervailing centers tend to develop to contend against the old or new centers of concentration. The possession of power is neither moral nor immoral. The use of power, however, may be moral or immoral, just or unjust. It is a basic assumption of the editor of this book that racial oppression is unnecessary, immoral, and unjust. However, I do not assume that black, brown, or white people are more or less moral, more or less immoral. Each has the capacity to abuse power and to enhance personhood. I selected scholars representing many disciplines in the behavioral sciences and humanities who have observed these facts of life for different racial groups and who have called them as they saw them.

While the language of baseball is used in referring to the straightforward analyses of many of our authors, I do not consider race relations in the United States to be a game. Our failure to discover ways of reconciling the races could result in the undoing of all of our communities. And such a process would not be very humorous, as the closing years of the 1960 decade revealed. In the 1970s it is possible that our society either will experience the institutional change that will usher in an increased sense of community or will come to know in a concrete way the misery of social disorganization and chaos.

In an attempt to deal with the realities of race relations, this book begins by defining the problem in all of its ugly aspects, including the suspicions, fears, distrust, and even hostilities that members of minority groups—particularly the people in black and brown populations—have experienced and expressed in recent years. It continues by showing how these feelings of resentment and mistrust have resulted in disunity among potential allies who need the help of each other to contend against the strong power centers of oppression. The book clearly labels the oppression that continues to be visited upon black and brown racial populations as _institutional racism._ Thus, socially sanctioned means are used to exclude some people from access to the opportunities of this society that ought to be available to all. The book indicates how difficult it is to identify patterns of institutional oppression because the people who abide by the oppressive social norms may be without personal malice toward individuals who are discriminated against in a lawful way. Although the mechanism of oppression may appear to be legitimate, the consequence ultimately is disquieting and disruptive. Apparently, injustice cannot be socially regulated and contained forever.

In a discussion of strategies for social action, the book leans heavily upon the methods of community development. The advocates of this approach contend that the benefits that flow from social organization and collective efforts are human rights and are not privileges to be extended or denied in an arbitrary and capricious way. The community-development approach emphasizes self-determination, and conflict when necessary, as a way of accommodating competing claims. Controlled conflict without violence probably is best achieved in the political institutional system of a community that is designed to effect compromises and trade-offs. This book describes how racial minorities have seized power in this area. It also demonstrates that concentrations of power among black, brown, or white people will tend to stimulate countervailing movements for the purpose of wresting power from the controlling agents. This struggle is probably eternal and is neither moral nor immoral. What a healthy society needs is a sufficient amount of openness that will facilitate continuous challenges to concentrated power in a way that enhances the powerful and the less powerful. Effective groups that challenge the centers of concentrated power also need flexible methods of operating, including aggressiveness, cooperation, and withdrawal. The conditions under which one approach is more or less effective are briefly illustrated in this book, but much more research is needed. The less-powerful racial populations tend to react to the majority populations in a way that is as stereotyped as the way the majority relates to the minority. Stereotyped reactions often are inappropriate for achieving intended goals. A flexible approach is desirable in which the methods and techniques employed are in terms of the requirements of the situation.

Finally, the book closes with an epilogue—a parable of the self-reliant woman and the self-righteous man. In the parable, there are images of the sexual basis of some of our hang-ups, racial and otherwise. But more than this, the parable is a commentary on the futility of attempting to solve a public and institutional problem with a private and personal approach. Such an approach not only may be useless but eventually may be damaging to all as well.

References

1. Frazier, E. Franklin. 1939, 1948, 1966. *The Negro Family in the United States.* Chicago: University of Chicago Press.
2. Frazier, E. Franklin. 1957. *The Negro in the United States.* New York: Macmillan.
3. Griffin, John Howard. 1960. *Black Like Me.* New York: New American Library.
4. Hill, Robert. 1972. *The Strengths of the Black Family.* New York: Emerson Hall.
5. Jackson, Maynard H. 1974. "Speech at Campaign Kickoff Luncheon." *Morehouse College Bulletin* 42 (Spring).
6. Merton, Robert. 1972. "Insiders and Outsiders: A Chapter in the Sociology of Knowledge." *American Journal of Sociology* 78 (July).
7. Myrdal, Gunnar. 1944. *An American Dilemma.* New York: Harper and Brothers.
8. Parsons, Talcott. 1948. "Max Weber's Sociological Analysis of Capitalism and Modern Institutions." In *An Introduction to the History of Sociology.* Edited by Harry Elmer Barnes. Chicago: University of Chicago Press.
9. Pettigrew, Thomas F. 1973. "Racism and the Mental Health of White Americans: A Social-Psychological View." In *Racism and Mental Health.* Edited by Charles V. Willie, Bernard Kramer, and Bertram Brown. Pittsburgh, Pa.: University of Pittsburgh Press.
10. Redding, J. Saunders. 1962. *On Being Negro in America.* Indianapolis, Ind.: Bobbs-Merrill.
11. United States Department of Labor. 1965. *The Negro Family, A Case for National Action.* Washington, D.C.: U.S. Government Printing Office.
12. Willie, Charles V., and Levy, Joan. 1972. "Black Is Lonely on White Campuses." *Psychology Today*, March.
13. Willie, Charles V., and McCord, Arline. 1972. *Black Students at White Colleges.* New York: Praeger.

Black/Brown/White Relations

I

Definitions
of the Problem

Suspicion, Distrust,
and Hostility

Alienation and Estrangement

Interethnic Group Disunity

Institutional Racism

Overview

Suspicion, fear, distrust, and hostility are the probable products of the 1970s that are directly traceable to the rising expectations but dashed hopes for black and brown people during the 1960s. It is well that the nation should prepare itself to endure more alienation, estrangement, and a general deterioration in race relations associated with these moods. Alienation has been appropriately characterized as a failure in relationships between the individual and society.

The year of the March on Washington, there was hope. A national poll conducted then by Louis Harris found that two-thirds of the black people in the United States believed that the attitudes of whites would be better in about five years. More than a decade later, this hope has not been experienced. In fact, the Rev. Dr. Martin Luther King, Jr., the esteemed leader of poor black people, was assassinated. His death ended a beautiful nonviolent, protest movement.

Moreover, the gap between whites and blacks continues and has widened in some areas. The median income for whites, for example, continues to be thirty-five to forty-five percent higher than the median for blacks. Desegregation in public education, which was for the purpose of obtaining equality for all racial groups, has slowed down to a snail's pace. Affirmative-action programs designed to redress the injustices of the past by laying an extraordinary requirement upon employers to seek out workers in black and brown racial minority groups are being challenged as an unfair practice against whites. The War on Poverty has ended, without victory for the poor.

As pointed out in testimony before the Commission on Population Growth and the American Future (included in this book under the title "A National Population Policy and the Fear of Racial Genocide"), blacks believe that America is capable of practicing genocide against them as Germany did against Jews.

From a social-science perspective, then, the era of Martin Luther King, Jr. from the Montgomery Bus Boycott to his death was decisive in American history. It changed the structure of relationships among the races. Before the boycott, many blacks believed that the burden was theirs to justify why they should be accepted. After King's death, in the minds of many blacks, the burden shifted to whites to justify any form of rejection. For in Martin Luther King, Jr. blacks believed they had met every requirement for their full participation in society.

Whites, in particular, have not understood the significance of this decisive period and are confused when blacks insist on participating in social organizations as a human right and not as a privilege to be granted or withdrawn, at will. The thirteen-year era of Martin Luther King, Jr. witnessed the beginning of nonnegotiable demands and the end of self-blame for deficiencies and failures.

Probably the best example of this new orientation was the way in which the Moynihan Report on the black family was soundly rejected. Blacks rejected the assertion by Moynihan that their family structure had seriously retarded their progress because it was out of line with the rest of American society. Before the era of King, blacks were inclined to bring any form of behavior deviant from that of whites in line with that of whites. But during the demonstrations led by Martin Luther King, Jr., blacks learned to be themselves, to engage in creative dissent, and to resist all attempts to be made over in the image of whites. Blacks still believe that it is fine and beautiful to claim that they are made in the image of God. But to be made in the image of whites is something else—something for which they do not aspire. In the past, the racial minorities tried to make themselves acceptable so that they might be accepted. Now they are demanding acceptance on their own terms, and they do not tolerate rejection lightly.

Whites, in turn, resist these demands, which are new and novel. Whites do not understand largely because they are the dominant people of power in America who used to give the orders. Thus, a standoff relationship now exists between the combined populations of black and brown people on the one hand and white people on the other. It is a confusing situation for blacks as well as for whites. The etiquette of race relations is all mixed up. Many whites still act as if they were superior but few blacks now believe that they are inferior. New patterns of race relations are just beginning to evolve.

Jewelle Taylor Gibbs in her chapter on "Black Students at Integrated Colleges" states that the emotional trauma in integrated settings is particularly severe for black females. Minority students, in general, have little trust in white institutions. Black females especially have feelings of depression, anger, or hostility. These feelings appear to result from the evolution of new interracial structures experienced by blacks and whites participating in common institutions and having more interracial contact than in the past. But the races seem to have developed a mistrust of each other in the process.

Because of rising expectations and unfulfilled hopes, David Owens relates that the anger is mounting in blacks. He marvels at John Williams, a black writer and author of *The Man Who Cried I Am*, who sustained high-pitched and intense anger for more than 400 pages. In his novel, Williams wanders through unsatisfying episodes of interracial sex, frustrations, betrayal, lynchings—symbolic and real —and finally to the realization that genocide is a possibility. Williams is really angry and he is not alone. Owens tells us that among angry blacks, whites are seen as being worse than barbarians.

The anger of blacks, and particularly black women, is further reflected in Linda J. M. LaRue's analysis of "Black Liberation and Women's Lib." She, too, urges blacks not to imitate whites and exhibits an abiding distrust of all majority-group members, females as well as males. One reason why few black women are actively involved in the women's liberation movements, LaRue states, is due to the absence of any guarantee that free white women will act differrently from free white men.

There is a possibility that LaRue may have underestimated the suffering and oppression of white women and overestimated the power and freedom of white men. This kind of error is to be expected when no common ground is recognized that may bind together oppressed groups of the same sex but of different races. When the behavior of the majority is stereotyped, cognitive differentiation is cast out and similarities between dominants and subdominants are ignored. Also, alliances—the strength of mass movements—are not effected when mutuality of goal and experience is denied. Opportunity for concerted action is missed when two or more groups assert that among them there can be no common cause. But such is the outcome of anger and hostility when found among blacks and browns as well as whites.

Fred Barbaro in his chapter, "Ethnic Resentment," indicates that the distrust, alienation, and estrangement between racial and ethnic groups have prevented the formation of effective coalitions even among populations who have recognized a common experience of discrimination. He describes the racial minority groups, especially the blacks, Puerto Ricans, and Mexican Americans, as turning inward and having a period of ethnocentric preoccupation. These groups, however, are not totally to blame. Indeed the author accuses conservative forces within the U.S. Congress of implementing anti-poverty programs in ways that would guarantee the conflict that has been observed. Thus, the distrust that characterizes relations among the groups mentioned has been aided and abetted by legislation and other institutional means.

This conclusion is reinforced by the findings of Ann H. Beuf in a study of "Racial Attitudes of Native-American Preschoolers." She sees institutional patterns, rather than painful personal experience with prejudice, as the major factor in influencing the racial preference of minority-group children. She hypothesizes that the way to develop positive attitudes among Native-American children toward their own race is by providing them with a view of society in which the hierarchy of power is not correlated with race. W. Curtis Banks, Janet L. Hubbard, and Joseph S. Vannoy, studying prejudice among whites, come to a similar conclusion that "many forms of prejudice are elicited and maintained by situational factors such as implicit social norms."

This means that the fear, anger, and hostility so debilitating to the members of racial minority groups require changes in the social system as well as within groups and individuals to overcome the limitations imposed by these moods. Nijole Benokraitis and Joe Feagin have prepared a fine chapter on this topic that is entitled "Institutional Racism: A Perspective in Search of Clarity and Research." They state that a systematic study of norms, roles, and statuses that are responsible for structuring institutions (as opposed to a study of individuals and their attitudes) would make a major contribution to our understanding of racial inequality and would provide far-reaching policy implications for ways of achieving racial reconciliation during the decades ahead.

1

A National Population Policy
and the Fear of Racial Genocide*

Charles V. Willie

Some people in the black community are deeply suspicious of any family-planning program initiated by whites. Whites probably have heard about but not taken seriously the call by some male-dominated black militant groups for black females to eschew the use of contraceptives because they are pushed in the black community as "a method of exterminating black people." While black females often take a different view about contraceptives than their male militant companions, they are also concerned about the possibility of black genocide in America.

The genocidal charge is neither "absurd" nor "hollow," as some whites have contended. It is also not limited to residents of the ghetto, whether they are young black militants or middle-aged black moderates. Indeed, my own studies of black students at white colleges indicate that young educated blacks fear black genocide, too (11).

This statement from a black female student is representative of the thinking of so many other blacks. She said: "The institutions in society are so strong. The C.I.A. is everywhere. I believe that America desires to perpetuate concentration camps for political

*This is a revised version of a paper presented before the Commission on Population Growth and the American Future, Washington, D.C., 13 April 1971.

opponents of the system of this country. People who speak out against the system are being systematically cut down." She concluded her recitation of despair with this depressing thought: "I wouldn't say that this society is against all-out genocide for black people" (11, p. 7). While there is uncertainty in her accusation, there is no mood of hope.

I designate the death of Martin Luther King, Jr. as the beginning of this serious concern among blacks about the possibility of genocide in America. There were lynchings, murders, and manslaughters in the past. But the assassination of Dr. King was too much. Many blacks believed that Dr. King had represented their best. He was scorned, spat upon, and slain. If America could not accept Dr. King, then many felt that no black person in America was safe. For none other could match the magnificent qualities of this great man. Yet his achievements and character were not enough. So he was cut down by the bullet of a white assassin, in a crime that remains mysterious when considering the help that the assassin received in escaping to a foreign land.

I dwell upon this event of our modern history because the Commission on Population Growth and the American Future must consider the present as well as the recent past, which is the context within which it must plan for the future. This context cannot be ignored. The American society must assure black people that it is committed to their survival with dignity and equality. The Commission on Population Growth must demonstrate that participation in any national plan will serve the self-interests of blacks.

The Commission will have difficulty demonstrating that a national population policy will fulfill the self-interests of black people. To some blacks, any call today by a federal commission for a national population policy, especially if it focuses on family planning, sounds similar to a call some years ago by a federal official for a national program to stabilize the black family. That call was set forth in *The Negro Family, A Case for National Action*, which was prepared by the U.S. Labor Department (10). Its chief author was Daniel Patrick Moynihan. I need not remind you of the negative reaction of blacks to the Moynihan Report. Many blacks got the idea that the national policy Moynihan was advocating was designed to make over blacks in the image of whites. They got this idea from his allegation that the matriarchal family structure that exists among blacks has seriously retarded their progress *"because it is so out of line with the rest of the American society* (10, p. 29, italics added). In an article published later in *Daedalus*, Moynihan described the black family as being in a state of "unmistakable crisis." He concluded that the crisis was acute because of "the *extraordinary rise* in Negro population" (7, p. 299, italics added).

While Moynihan may not have intended to give this impression these two statements seem, to me, to call for a national policy to obliterate any family forms among blacks that might be different from the family forms found among whites. Moreover, he suggested that the nation should act quickly to refurbish blacks in the image of whites because blacks were gaining on whites in numbers. These statements came from someone who has been an intimate consultant to presidents. Blacks were suspicious of Moynihan's call for a national policy that focused upon the black family. The Moynihan Report, therefore, is excess baggage that the Commission (or any other national planning and policy-recommending group) does not need and from which it should separate itself.

If the Commission on Population Growth and the American Future is to promulgate a national policy that will gain the cooperation of black people, such a policy must fulfill the goals and aspirations that blacks themselves have identified as important. A national population policy must demonstrate that it is more concerned about the *health* and *wealth* of black people than it is about the number of children they have.

Let me explain why some blacks believe that a national population policy that focuses upon limiting the number of black children born is a desperation move on the part of whites to remain in control. Whites were not concerned about the size and structure of black families a century ago. Then blacks were nearly one-fifth (18.4 percent) of the total population. This, of course, was during the age of slavery in the 1820s. Then blacks were not free. They were not a challenge to whites. Although they represented one out of every five persons in the United States, and although the family assumed even more functions for the growth, development, and well-being of individuals then, than it probably does today, American whites were not concerned about the fertility or stability of the black family at that point in time. Indeed, there were attempts to breed healthy black male slaves with healthy black female slaves, disregarding any family connections and, in many instances, even prohibiting marriage. Gunnar Myrdal wrote, "most slave owners. . .did not care about the marital state of their slaves. . .[in fact,] the internal slave trade broke up many slave families" (8, p.931). Neither the size of the black population nor its circumstances of family life worried white Americans before black people were free.

But with the emergence of the Freedom Movement among blacks, there is a continuing call for self-determination. White Americans have become concerned about the size, the structure, and the stability of the black family. Moynihan alerted blacks about what was in the minds of some whites when he described the situation as "acute" because of the "extraordinary rise in Negro population." The size, structure, and stability of the black family were of no concern to some white Americans when black people were enslaved. The size, structure, and stability of the black family are cause for alarm among some white Americans, requiring a national program of control, now that black people are beginning to achieve freedom and equality.

Blacks, of course, would not claim that there has been an extraordinary rise in their population. Blacks in America have increased from 9.9 percent in 1920 to approximately 11.4 percent in the early 1970s—hardly "extraordinary." But then maybe an increase of between one and two percentage points of the total population is an extraordinary rise if one believes it is. Sociologist Robert Merton has written that "self-hypnosis through one's own propaganda is a not infrequent phase of the self-fulfilling prophecy" (4, p. 185).

Moreover, a population increase of one to two percentage points of the total creates an "acute" situation and is cause for alarm if the ultimate national goal is to eliminate black people; for such an increase, although small, indicates that they will not go away.

The genocidal fears of blacks, therefore, are anchored in facts. These facts are: (1) that a leading governmental spokesman declared that an increase of black people of one to two percentage points of the total population is "extraordinary"; (2) that over the years the greatest contributor to family instability among blacks has been the death of the male spouse rather than divorce or desertion; and (3) that the major control upon the fertility rate of blacks in the past has been the deaths of their very young children.

Back in 1910, twenty-seven percent of black females were members of broken families because their husbands were dead. During that same year, only six percent of black families were broken because of divorce or desertion of the male spouse. Thus death was four times more frequently a contributor to family disruption than other social causes. I should add that death of the husband was the chief cause for marital breakup for black families compared with desertion or divorce as late as 1963. Thus divorce and desertion, which were highlighted by Moynihan as reasons why a national program to stabilize the black family was needed, are newcomers as chief causes of family breakup for black people. The information on trends in marital status comparing the relative contributions of death, desertion, and divorce to family breakup among blacks was obtained from findings by Reynolds Farley (2, p. 175).

It would seem that whites were not concerned about the stability of the black family when it was broken largely because black men were dying prematurely. Whites now are concerned about the size, structure, and stability of the black family when the number of black men who are dying prematurely is decreasing and the number of black live-born children who survive is increasing.

Irene Tauber, a distinguished demographer, has said that "the test of future population policies, planned and unplanned, will be in the speed and the completeness of the obliteration of those demographies that can be categorized by the color of the skin or the subcultures of origin" (9, p. 37). A national population policy cannot succeed if it focuses only on reproduction and family size of one category of people. Past experiences have revealed that family planning, particularly with reference to size, is often a function of other socioeconomic opportunities. Clyde Kiser and Myrna Frank have discovered that black women over twenty-five years of age who have a college education or who are married to professional men tend to have a fertility rate that is much lower than that for whites of similar circumstances (3, pp. 42-43). Irene Tauber also refers to the socioeconomic facts of life. She states that "trends in the fertility of the blacks in future years will be influenced both by rapidity of the upward economic and social movements and by that complex of factors that influences national fertility, white or black. . ." (9, p. 37). It can be stated, in general, that an inverse relationship exists between fertility and socioeconomic status factors. People of higher income, occupation, and education tend to have fewer children.

However, the association between fertility and socioeconomic factors is a bit more complex when one is dealing with blacks. Reynolds Farley relates that among urban blacks a general increase in fertility has occurred that has involved all social classes. He concludes that this is probably due to improved health conditions resulting in decreased death rates, particularly infant and maternal mortality (1, pp. 189, 194-95).

These facts should help the Commission understand why some blacks who only recently have begun to receive the kind of health care that whites have received for years are lukewarm to any discussions about reducing fertility when they have begun to exhibit modest gains in fertility only because of increased health care. Because so little trust exists among the races in the United States, when whites speak of limiting fertility or controlling the family in any way, many blacks believe that these whites wish to return to a modified Malthusian plan that has controlled black family life in the past. Blacks know that their families have been disrupted and limited in the past because of deaths. They, therefore, are suspicious of any program that does not assure them that death again will not be the chief controlling variable.

In a jocular vein, Moynihan, writing for *America* magazine, the National Catholic Weekly Review, said, "while the rich of America do whatever it is they do, the poor are begetting children" (6, p. 392). I should point out in a not so jocular vein that many of the children begotten by the black poor in the past died before reaching manhood or womanhood and that children begotten by these blacks today are beginning to live, so that the proportion of black people in the total population is increased by one to two percentage points of the total. The increase in fertility due to these achievements in health care therefore is no cause for alarm. Indeed, the Commission on Population Growth should urge and encourage a fertility that is not impeded by disease and death.

If the poor beget children, if the number they beget is counter-productive for the future welfare of the total nation, and if there is an inverse association between fertility and socioeconomic status, then it would seem that a national population policy should have as a major plank a program to guarantee equality in economic and educational opportunities for all people in this nation. This means that a national population policy must come out strongly against racial and ethnic discrimination. Herman Miller of the U.S. Census Bureau offers that "the average Negro earns less than the average white, even when he has the same years of schooling and does the same kind of work." This conclusion comes from the analysis of income figures that, according to Miller, "provide the unarguable evidence on which public policy should rest" (5, p. 21).

It is for this reason that I conclude that a national population policy that would serve the best interests of blacks as well as the other citizens of this nation should focus on enhancing the *health* and *wealth* of every household in America as well as controlling family size, structure, and stability.

References

1. Farley, Reynolds. 1970. "Fertility among Urban Blacks." *Milbank Memorial Fund Quarterly* 48, part 2 (April).
2. Farley, Reynolds. 1970. "Trends in Marital Status among Blacks." In *The Family Life of Black People*. Edited by Charles V. Willie. Columbus, Ohio: Merrill.
3. Kiser, Clyde V., and Frank, Myrna E. 1970. "Factors Associated with Low Fertility of Nonwhite Women of College Attainment." In *The Family Life of Black People*. Edited by Charles V. Willie. Columbus, Ohio: Merrill.
4. Merton, Robert. 1949. *Social Theory and Social Structure*. New York: Free Press.
5. Miller, Herman. 1964. *Rich Man, Poor Man*. New York: Crowell.
6. Moynihan, Daniel P. 1967. "A Family Policy for the Nation." In *The Moynihan Report and the Politics of Controversy*. Edited by Lee Rainwater and William L. Yancy. Cambridge, Mass.: MIT Press.
7. Moynihan, Daniel P. 1970. "The Ordeal of the Negro Family." In *The Family Life of Black People*. Edited by Charles V. Willie. Columbus, Ohio: Merrill.
8. Myrdal, Gunnar. 1944. *The American Dilemma*. New York: Harper and Brothers.
9. Tauber, Irene. 1970. "Discussion at Milbank Memorial Fund Roundtable on Demographic Aspects of the Black Community." *Milbank Memorial Fund Quarterly* 48, part 2 (April).
10. United States Department of Labor. 1965. *The Negro Family, A Case for National Action*. Washington, D.C.: U.S. Government Printing Office.
11. Willie, Charles V., and McCord, Arline. 1972. *Black Students at White Colleges*. New York: Praeger.

2

Black Students at Integrated Colleges: Problems and Prospects

Jewelle Taylor Gibbs

The most significant event in recent years that focused the attention of the educational establishment on the inequities of the educational process was the assassination of Martin Luther King, Jr. One of the unintended consequences of this tragic event was the momentum gained by the nascent black-student movement, whose leaders seized upon King's martyrdom as a symbolic lever to press for admission of larger numbers of black students to higher education, a greater diversity of backgrounds and educational experiences among the recruited, increased financial aid, and improved educational services, cultural facilities, and counseling for black students accepted.

This chapter will examine some of the issues involved in the mutual adaptation of black students to predominantly white colleges and universities, the range of psychological and social problems experienced by these students, and the patterns of adaptation developed by the students in order to cope with their minority status.

The analysis of the issues, problems, and adaptive solutions developed by black students at integrated universities has developed as the result of my experience as a psychiatric social worker and counselor at two San Francisco Bay Area universities. The major substantive ideas delineated in this chapter have been previously published or presented elsewhere (5, 6, 7, 8). They are synthesized here and formulations are developed that are applicable to a broad spectrum of black students and a variety of integrated institutions.

Issues of Mutual Adaptation

In a survey designed to evaluate the attitudes of black undergraduates and their modes of adaptation to their experiences at Stanford University, I found that the major concerns of the students participating in the survey were in the areas of academic performance, social and extracurricular activities, interracial relationships, and financial matters (5). While the majority of these students had attended integrated high schools, there was a wide-spread feeling of alienation from the white students and complaints about the predominantly white middle-class atmosphere of the campus and surrounding community. Anxiety about academic competition, uncertainty about financial sources, insecurity over involvement in social and extracurricular activities—all of these constant pressures resulted in feelings of ambivalence among the students and tension between the students and the administrators.

Robert Coles, in a paper describing the attitudes of Harvard students who felt racially, culturally, or politically distinct from the majority of their fellow students, pointed out the defensiveness and bitterness of the black students who perceived their racial identity as a barrier to effective adjustment to the campus community (2). Hammond's analysis of minority students at the University of Virginia points out that they are "in the limbo of transition from one class to another and from one subculture to another...," resulting in the development of a syndrome he refers to as *cultural paranoia* (9).

Martin Kilson of Harvard University has crystallized the issue of racial-cultural conflicts for black students in white institutions in the following quote: "Since 1971, the pressures for conformity to black-solidarity behavior have been well-nigh overwhelming at Harvard. Only the most individualistic Negro students—a distinct minority—have been able to withstand them. The pressures have had, moreover, a profound emotional impact on Negro students, producing deep-seated emotional ambivalence and instability. To whom do Negro students owe primary loyalty? The demands of black-solidarity forces, or the academic and intellectual processes of Harvard College?" (10).

The black students have countered with assertions that they were forced into these patterns by the patronizing attitudes, discriminatory acts, misguided liberalism, or outright indifference of their fellow white students, faculty, and staff. Moreover, many students felt that they did not want to surrender their sense of ethnic identity in order to adapt to the majority culture. In a thoughtful rejoinder to Kilson's comments on Harvard blacks, a group of students offered a contrasting viewpoint:

> He [Kilson] genuinely believes, it seems, that there is no significance in cultural blackness unless it apes or imitates white cultural norms every step of the way. We submit that such an absurd and total mimicry by blacks of the dominant American culture would not only be antithetical to the purported American ideal of cultural pluralism, but also (and more so) antithetical to every natural and human inclination toward love of self. . . .There can be no justifiable reason why blacks at Harvard, or anywhere else, should be made to negate those qualities in ourselves that render us distinct from the mass, while simultaneously affirming its existence. Black people in this country have a certain important perception; this input and perception cannot possibly be pathological, since they have provided us with the necessary prowess to survive within a hostile American environment for over four hundred years. And they have been an input and perception that have provided this nation with conscience, and humor, and rhythm, and beauty. (13)

In a survey of black Stanford University undergraduates, Dean Harold Boyd found that academic issues were of major concern to the group. Advising is essential for black students because they often come from families that are unfamiliar with college life and are therefore unable to provide meaningful advice or counsel concerning major fields and future careers (1).

Social life and interpersonal relationships between blacks and whites and among the black students themselves is another major issue for students and administrators. As long as there were only a handful of blacks on predominantly white campuses, they tended to merge into integrated social and extracurricular activities. This was true during the fifties and early sixties when black students often led dual social lives, that is, participating in the general campus social life while simultaneously joining black sororities and fraternities, attending black churches and social functions in surrounding communities, and developing a network of other black contacts. Because their numbers were small on the individual campuses, there was never an issue about separatism, although there were undoubtedly innumerable instances when blacks did not feel particularly welcome.

More recently with the advent of larger groups of blacks on integrated campuses, patterns of social separation have developed with justifications based on arguments ranging from innate racial preferences to racial exclusion by whites. These patterns have culminated in the demands for separate dormitories, separate eating facilities, separate lounges for study and recreational purposes, and separate facilities for cultural activities.

Not only has the black-student population increased in size during the past decade, but it has also increased in heterogeneity; that is, students from all socioeconomic levels, family backgrounds, and cultural attitudes are now attending college. Although the mass media have focused on the issue of black-white relationships on integrated campuses, there has been as much friction and tension between the various groups of black students, sometimes because of class differences, and sometimes because of differences in cultural outlook, intellectual interests, and recreational pursuits.

The financial issue continues to be of major significance to black students and university administrators. Black students often discover that the financial aid they have been granted is hardly sufficient to cover all their most basic educational expenses, which may necessitate getting a part-time job or a loan. Since many students are also educationally disadvantaged when they enter college, the need to work for extra funds may be detrimental to their academic work. As universities have had to rein in their total budgets, they have shown less willingness to invest money in minority students and have required those students to demonstrate more personal initiative and motivation in obtaining funds from other sources, even though these sources are also drying up.

Finally, the issue of ideology is of paramount importance in its own right, and in its interstitial influence on all the other issues. One of the popular phrases that characterized the rhetoric of the black-student movement of the early seventies exhorted blacks to "define ourselves for ourselves" by "telling it like it is" and "taking care of business." This new image of blackness, fostered by the identification with the African-nationalist movement and the evolution of the civil-rights movement into a more militant black-power orientation, emphasized the cultural heritage of African and Caribbean roots, revived interest in Afro-American contributions to American and world history, espoused community control of black ghettos and black institutions, and advocated economic and political autonomy for black communities. Notwithstanding the positive concepts embedded in the new black ideology, there were some negative consequences in terms of attitudes, behavior, and aspirations that will be described at length later.

What was the effect of this new ideology on black students in integrated colleges? The students translated the ideological concepts into specific programmatic activities, primarily through the vehicle of the black-student unions that mushroomed throughout the country during the late sixties. Black-student organizations focused on changes in admissions policies to increase the number and variety of black students in the student population, to nurture improvements in student services and counseling facilities to address the needs of blacks, to develop courses and programs dealing with Afro-American studies, and to establish black cultural and social programs and facilities. Another facet of this activity focused on the improvement of relationships between black students and blacks in the surrounding communities, for example, providing volunteers for tutoring, working in poverty programs, and developing other community improvement programs, political campaigns, and economic revitalization.

Expectations of Black Students and White Administrators

As the number of black students on white campuses has increased in recent years, it has become evident that their expectations about university life and their role in it were often quite different from and incompatible with the expectations of the white administrators and faculty members. First, administrators and faculty expected that the black students would be assimilated into the university community without significant alteration of the structure or programs of the university. Second, the faculty was not prepared to deal with the academic deficiencies of some students from substandard, ghetto high schools. In other cases, faculty members tended to generalize from initial experiences with a few unprepared students who did not want to be patronized or treated as if they were handicapped.

Third, problems relating to interpersonal relationships between blacks and whites, among blacks of different backgrounds, interracial dating, dormitory life, and extracurricular activities were often underestimated or unanticipated by the staff. On many campuses black students developed their own social and cultural organizations, modeled after quasi-political groups, which served a multiplicity of purposes for a variety of student needs—from group therapy to political consciousness raising. For those students who felt culturally alien and politically alienated from the white majority, these black organizations served as a channel for their discontent as well as their fears and hostilities.

Fourth, university officials expected that black students would be grateful for the opportunity to obtain a quality education at a four-year integrated institution. They expected that this gratitude would express itself in conformity to the norms, acceptance of the status quo, and allegiance to the university community. Thus, they were not prepared to deal with student unrest, criticism, or attempts to change the status quo, even though this indicated a healthy autonomy among black students. In a very subtle fashion, this expectation of university officials reflected a latent paternalism.

Fifth, university officials apparently expected black students to function successfully without the support system of the black community, although many of them were reared in extended families and neighborhoods with a network of affiliations. The fact that they would be on predominantly white campuses that, in most instances, were quite isolated from inner-city neighborhoods and from institutions that served the black community, as well as from services that were geared to the black consumer market (for example, beauty products, barbers and beauticians, publications, restaurants, and the like), was not adequately evaluated as a potential problem.

Student expectations, by contrast, were perhaps not as clearly explicit or articulated as were the expectations of the administrators and faculty. However, some expectations were apparent and others can be inferred from the behavior and attitudes expressed by black students on a number of campuses, in the mass media, and in professional papers. First, their primary expectation was that the institution would be very flexible in responding to their individual needs, partly because some of them had been recruited with promises of unlimited academic and financial assistance, and partly because their previous experience with community organizations and institutions had often reinforced particularistic rather than universalistic criteria in the transaction of business. Thus, they had not learned how to negotiate the bureaucratic process, and they fully expected to bypass rules, obtain unlimited financial aid, and have their minor academic and social disputes settled by administrators, who were further expected to apply particularistic criteria in their decisions. When these expectations were not fulfilled promptly, the students expressed frustration and hostility toward the staff.

Second, students often expected college courses to be quite similar to high-school work, and they were quite confused by the qualitative and quantitative differences in courses and study assignments.

Third, black students had expected a greater diversity of activities and life-styles on white campuses. Their social and recreational interests reflected their own cultural milieu, so they were sometimes unfamiliar with the interests, values, and behavior patterns of other students. However, their concern for establishing a distinct ethnic identity by wearing Afro hairstyles, African outfits and mod clothes, eating soul food, and playing funky music was often more symbolic than genuine. A superficial cohesiveness among the students was fostered by these symbols of black identity, while simultaneously dramatizing their uniqueness on campus.

Fourth, black students expected to contribute as much to the university community as it contributed to them, that is, that there would be a mutual benefit to both groups from their inclusion in the student population. Students expressed their opinion that their presence on campus served as evidence of the university's commitment to education of the disadvantaged in our society, as a vehicle for diversifying the student body, and as a means of producing more trained minority leaders who could address themselves to the multiple problems of an interracial society. Thus, the students did not simply perceive of their role as the recipients of noblesse-oblige policies of white universities, but as partners in an educational venture that could benefit from occasional criticism and pressure for change.

Fifth, students expected to have greater contact with black communities located in the vicinity of their campuses. Students were often eager to socialize with other blacks, and to affiliate themselves with black social, civic, and religious organizations, but these contacts were not easy to make or maintain due to the problems of transportation, academic scheduling pressures, and differences in priorities between the students and the community leaders. The dilemma was further exacerbated by negative attitudes of the black community toward the local college or university because of prior town-grown conflicts or a policy of benign neglect of the university in its insensitivity to the needs of the community. These negative attitudes toward the institution were often generalized to the black students, frequently resulting in poor communication, hostile feelings, and strained relationships between community people and students. Thus, black students often found themselves in a double-bind situation, that is, frustrated at the lack of ties with the black community when they were not easily accessible, and still frustrated in their attempts to obtain meaningful and mutually constructive relationships when they did manage to make initial contacts.

The disparity between two sets of expectations—the assumptions of the university staff and the misconceptions of the black students— has led to a number of conflicts and confrontations on campuses throughout the country during the last decade. In evaluating the wide chasm between the expectations of these groups, one is led to conclude that this chasm is the major factor in the frequent communication breakdowns between the two groups, leading to misperceptions of each other's priorities, strategies, and goals. Black-student groups presented nonnegotiable demands for black studies departments, black dormitories and cultural centers, in- creased financial aid, additional black faculty and staff, and recruitment of more minority students. University officials responded, through the shock of confrontation, with reasoned dialogue and slow-moving bureaucratic channels, but they were not negotiating with people who were accustomed to intellectual discourse and red tape. Campuses from Cornell University, where students armed with guns occupied administrative buildings, to San Francisco State College, where students and police engaged in pitched battles, witnessed a series of confrontations between black students and university administrators. Reports and photographs of disturbances at Harvard University, Berkeley, Antioch, Ohio State, Brandeis, University of Minnesota, University of Michigan, University of Washington, and dozens of smaller colleges were circulated by the mass media, creating widespread antagonism or ambivalence among all sectors of the community, but particularly among those conservative educators, college trustees, politicians, and wealthy donors who had been opposed to the liberalization of college- admissions policies in the first place.

In addition to these well-publicized confrontations, the disparity in expectations had other less visible consequences for the black students, for instance, their inability to integrate the different viewpoints exacerbated the issues previously noted, as well as integrating a range of social and psychological problems that they experienced in adapting to university life.

The following section will summarize the results of a three-year study of the utilization of mental-health services by black students at Stanford University, as an in-depth example of the types of problems encountered by black students at a predominantly white university (8). Since there have been very few published studies documenting these problems, it is not possible to make broad generalizations from this specific campus situation to other types of private and public colleges. However, the findings of this utilization survey are comparable to a survey recently completed at Yale University (4) and to data from a few other studies, as well as to nonclinical reports of student problems as described by black and white administrators, counselors, and students themselves.

Mental-health Problems of Black Students in Integrated Colleges

Stanford University is a prestigious private college with high academic standards located in the San Francisco Bay Area. Its population of black students expanded rapidly from approximately 70 in 1966-67 to 548 in 1971-72; this sudden growth of a group from a different racial and cultural background was accompanied by problems of academic, social, and psychological adaptation to the university milieu, as was witnessed in many other American colleges during this period.

During the three-year academic period from 1969-72, a total of 87 black students came to the Mental Health Clinic, most of them voluntarily, for counseling or brief therapy concerning an emotional crisis or longer-term psychological problem with which they were unable to cope effectively. Case records of the black-student users were analyzed to determine the following factors about this clinic subpopulation: utilization rates, demographic characteristics of users, presenting problems, duration of therapy, and reasons for terminating therapy.

Utilization Rates

The actual number of black students using the clinic remained remarkably stable during the entire period of study, while the proportion of users to the total black-student population decreased from a high of 10.2 percent in 1969 to 6.4 percent in 1972. During this same period, blacks increased from 2.9 percent of the total student population in 1969-70 to 4.7 percent in 1971-72. Thus, in 1969-70 blacks were overrepresented in the clinic population, while in the following two years they were underrepresented, but these differences were not statistically significant (see Table 1).

Table 1

Black Student Utilization of Mental Health Clinic: 1969-72

Year of Intake	Total Black Users	Percent Using Clinic	Percent Blacks in Student Body	Percent Blacks in Clinic Pop.
1969-70	35	10.2	2.9	3.7
1970-71	33	8.1	3.5	2.3
1971-72	35	6.4	4.7	2.8

Characteristics of Clinic Users

Undergraduates accounted for 72 percent and graduates for 28 percent of the users during this period. Freshman year was the period of greatest stress with 38 percent of the group first seeking help at this time, while 33 percent had their initial session as sophomores, 11 percent as juniors, and 18 percent as seniors. This was also true among graduate students with 58 percent registering during their first year, and the remaining 42 percent distributed fairly evenly throughout the second, third, fourth, and fifth years of graduate study.

Fifty-three percent of the total group of black users were women, as were 60 percent of the undergraduates and 38 percent of the graduate students. Undergraduate users ranged in age from 17-32, with a modal age of 19, while the modal age of the graduate users was 23 with a range from 21-38 years. Four of the undergraduate users were married, while seven of the graduate students were married and two were divorced.

The socioeconomic class distribution, based on the occupation of the student's father or head of household, was as follows: 25 percent from upper-middle class families, 44 percent from middle-class families, 16 percent from working-class families, and 15 percent from lower-class families (see Table 2). This distribution was almost identical for both undergraduate and graduate users, indicating that middle and upper-middle class students (combined class I and II) are overrepresented relative to their proportions in the total black-student population. The proportions of male and female users in the two upper classes were quite similar, while working-class males tended to be higher utilizers than females and lower-class females tended to be higher utilizers than lower-class males.

Table 2

Sex and Socioeconomic Status of Black Clinic Users: 1969-72

Socioeconomic Status of Black Users	Undergraduates Males	Undergraduates Females	Graduate Students Males	Graduate Students Females	Total Number of Clinic Users	Percent of Clinic Users	Percent of Total Black Student Population
Class I: Professional, semi-professional, and managerial	6	9	4	3	22	25	38.1
Class II: White-collar, technical, and small business owners	11	17	6	4	38	44	21.2
Class III: Skilled and semiskilled trades	7	4	2	1	14	16	23.2
Class IV: Unskilled laborers and domestics	2	7	3	1	13	15	17.5
Totals	26	37	15	9	87	100	100

Geographically, black students from the Southern and Midwestern states tended to be slightly overrepresented among clinic users, while students from the Northeastern and Western states tended to be slightly underrepresented, as compared with the proportions of these regions represented in the total black group.

Prior to their admission to Stanford, the black clinic users were predominantly from urban areas and had attended integrated schools, with 82 percent from medium to large cities and 18 percent from small towns or suburban areas. Approximately two-thirds of the undergraduate users had attended integrated high schools and one-third had attended predominantly black high schools. The majority of the graduate users had attended integrated colleges.

Presenting Problems of Clinic Users

The students exhibited a wide variety of emotional problems and complaints in their counseling sessions; these can be categorized into eight major areas: heterosexual relationships, interpersonal relationships, identity crises, academic anxieties, feelings of depersonalization, family problems, affective and psychosomatic complaints, and career concerns. Fears of homosexuality, suicidal thoughts and behavior, and alcohol and drug use or abuse were less frequently mentioned, thus they were not major concerns of this group of black students.

Forty-eight percent of the students complained of problems with the opposite sex. Black females expressed feelings of depression, anger, or hostility because they felt that black males were inattentive, insensitive to their needs for affection, and overly preoccupied with sexual concerns. Many of these young women felt there was a conflict because black males freely dated white females, while there were tremendous social pressures that hindered their equal access to white males. Black males, on the other hand, reported feelings of ambivalence toward black females, mixed motives in dating white females, and feelings of guilt and disloyalty toward their black peers because of these relationships.

Black females of all social classes, but particularly middle-class females, exhibited considerable naivete concerning sexual practices, birth-control methods, and venereal disease prevention. During this period four girls requested termination of their pregnancies, while several requested accurate information about contraception or venereal disease. There was some discussion among this group of women of male sexual exploitation and a hustling mentality among some of the black males, particularly the ones from lower-class backgrounds, who often persuaded their dates to exchange sexual favors for social engagements. Moreover, black males threatened black females with loss of their attention or affection by comparing them sexually to white females, whom they described as more receptive, aggressive, and imaginative.

Married graduate students complained of difficulties that usually stemmed directly from their status as students. For example, several male students complained that their wives demanded too much of their time and attention, were not sympathetic to their academic pressures, or did not share their ultimate goals. In three cases, the marriage was in difficulty because the husband felt he had outgrown his wife intellectually and socially; this was true of two female graduate students whose husbands did not have educational or occupational status to enable them to match their wives' upward mobility. For both spouses the pressures of limited time, limited money, and crowded living conditions aggravated the usual adjustment process of the early married years. Sexual incompatibility accounted for four cases, while friction over leisure-time activities, child-rearing practices, finances, and values were more common complaints. There were ten cases involving marital problems among both graduates and undergraduates.

Forty percent of the students complained of problems in their relations with other students, staff, or faculty members. Symptoms ranged from anxiety in most interpersonal exchanges to feelings of anger and hostility toward specific individuals or groups. Conflicts between students were reported more frequently by individuals who lived in dormitories with a high concentration of black students. In these dormitories, where black students dominated the social, political, and cultural activities, difficulties often occurred between people whose values, interests, and activities reflected different socio-economic backgrounds and life-styles. Thus, some black students had friction with white students, or with other black students, or were unable to get along with anyone who represented a different viewpoint.

Students in this group tended to perceive any difficulties of adjustment or communication with a white student as evidence of prejudice or racism. However, when difficulties occurred between two blacks, this was interpreted as a natural element of black culture, which presumably encourages "telling it like it is" and "letting it all hang out." However, natural or not, the frequency of interpersonal conflicts among some groups of black students was too severe for some students to resolve without professional counseling.

Relationships between middle- and working-class black students were often strained because of their generally disparate economic and cultural experiences, as well as their different attitudes toward black nationalism, toward campus life, and toward education as a pathway to future goals. Working-class students often attempted to put middle-class students on the defensive about their clothes, recreational interests, attitudes toward whites, and academic interests. Conversely, middle-class students employed more subtle ways of asserting their social superiority over the working-class group, for example, driving late model cars, wearing expensive mod clothes, selecting nonconcentration dormitories, and socializing in informal groups of their own, while simultaneously boycotting social and cultural activities sponsored by the Black Students' Union. However, the stresses caused by these interpersonal conflicts among black students served to intensify identity conflicts that were prevalent in this group.

Nearly half (46 percent) of the clinic users exhibited a syndrome of symptoms that were identified as ethnic-identity conflicts. These conflicts took two major forms among black students. Individuals from middle-class integrated or semiintegrated backgrounds tended to be defensive about their familiarity with the general culture, to express guilt over their material and cultural advantages, and to expiate this guilt by adopting stereotyped behavior, language, and values associated with the ghetto life-style. The students from working- or lower-class backgrounds, where exposure to the white world was limited and circumscribed, expressed their identity conflicts in feelings of inferiority vis-à-vis the dominant culture, anxiety about competing academically with other students, feelings that they were not welcome in campus social and extracurricular activities, and ambivalence toward middle-class black students who had learned to adapt to the university milieu.

The precipitating factor in seeking counseling for these students was usually their growing discomfort with the lack of congruence between their idealized notion of their personal identity and the alternative identity with which they were experimenting in response to peer pressure. The inability of the student to resolve his identity crisis by establishing a meaningful personal identity resulted in emotional distress, interpersonal problems, academic inadequacies, conflict with parents and family members, and confusion over basic values and future goals.

More than one-third (35 percent) of the students complained of academic problems, with anxiety described as the most common symptom; this anxiety interfered with the student's ability to concentrate, to study effectively, or to perform well on papers and exams. Most of the students who experienced academic difficulties attributed them to poor high-school preparation, poor study habits, and lack of self-confidence in their ability to compete with other Stanford students. Students who had been admitted under altered admission criteria in the Task Force Program were overrepresented in the user group; 25 percent of the Task Force students were clinic patients, but they represented only 5 percent of the total black-student population during this period.

Fewer of the graduate students focused on academic problems in treatment, but nine expressed conflicts with their instructors over racial attitudes, educational philosophy, or teaching techniques. For most of these students, other personal problems made it more difficult for them to concentrate on their academic work, and thus the constant threat of academic failure simply created a vicious cycle of anxiety and inability to cope with academic demands.

Nearly one-fourth (24 percent) of the students complained of problems with their parents or families, usually centering around the issues of autonomy, financial management, social activities, and sociopolitical attitudes and involvement. The majority of this group felt that there is a considerable generation gap in values about style of dress, social activities, and political opinions. Many middle-class students felt that their parents were too "bourgeois," too materialistic, and too conservative about the black-power movement. Middle-class students complained more frequently that their parents were trying to control them in the areas of academic and extracurricular (especially political) activities, while working-class students felt that their parents interfered more with their social and financial affairs. For the lower-class student the problem of independence from parental authority was complicated by the fact that he was often depriving the family of a much-needed additional income and creating greater financial and social strains for the whole family by staying in school. Moreover, in families where authoritarian child-rearing patterns had been practiced, the parents had not adequately prepared the child for the transition from adolescence to young adulthood, so it was often more difficult for these students to make independent judgments and to know how to evaluate the consequences of their actions. The lower-class black student was further handicapped in his drive for autonomy by two other characteristics of his subculture, that is, his circumscribed environment that usually did not afford him many opportunities for adapting to new situations and new people, and his extended family structure that emphasized collective priorities and goals rather than rewarding individual efforts to achieve or to differentiate oneself from the rest of the family unit.

Thus, the usual adolescent struggle for autonomy was heightened in those black students who must deal with the anxieties and fears of their parents concerning their specific ethnic roles vis-à-vis the expectations of society, as well as the obligations to their extended families. The anxieties of middle-class parents essentially revolved around academic and sociopolitical issues, focusing on the obligations of the child to capitalize on his educational opportunity and to avoid involvement in the black militant and radical-left student movements, while the anxieties of the working- and lower-class parents reflected their ambivalence toward the personal and financial autonomy and the intellectual sociocultural changes affecting their children and enhancing their chances for socioeconomic mobility. The students' search for independence from possessive, controlling, or rejecting parents resulted in symptoms of depression, apathy, or psychosomatic complaints.

Fourteen students complained of a syndrome of feelings and attitudes that included loneliness, sadness, apathy, alienation from other people, and loss of interest in studies. Prone to suicidal fantasies, these students felt that they were unloved by their families and unable to relate well to their peers, teachers, and friends. In general, they related a long history of chronic feelings of depression, loneliness, and isolation. Although these students represented only 16 percent of the black clinic users, their symptoms were quite similar to the expressed concerns of white students about the existentialist dilemma of contemporary society. For these black students the issue of ethnic identity was subsumed under the much broader issue of human identity, namely, the search for meaning in their lives.

Nearly three-fourths (74 percent) of the students complained of feelings of depression, anger, or anxiety. These feelings could usually be traced to problems in the other areas of social, personal, or academic adjustment. However, there were some students who were unable to relate their feelings to any situations or relationships, but reported that they were overwhelmed by pervasive anxiety, depression, or hostility, which had a debilitating effect on their ability to handle their normal tasks. As these generalized feelings were clarified in counseling sessions, students reported that they stemmed from feelings of inadequacy or inferiority, fears of failure or the possibility of disappointing their parents and families, inability to comprehend or cope with the many conflicting sets of pressures they felt as black students, and uncertainty about future opportunities and goals.

Psychosomatic complaints were registered by 25 percent of the students; these included sleep disturbances and a variety of symptoms involving the gastrointestinal, cardiopulmonary, or central nervous systems. These symptoms were apparently related to the same stresses that produced the feelings of depression or anxiety, but they occurred in students who had greater difficulties in expressing their feelings directly. They also tended to be more debilitating and continuous, while students who experienced affective complaints tended to suffer from episodic mood swings that did not produce physical manifestations.

About ten percent of the students expressed concern over their future plans. This group primarily sought information or vocational counseling, but a few were in conflict about career goals. Several of the graduate students faced the dilemma of teaching or working in a predominantly black setting versus competing for academic or occupational advancement in a predominantly white setting. Some felt ideologically committed to returning to the South to upgrade the black colleges and to improve the quality of life in black communities, yet they realized that this choice might ultimately restrict their professional advancement.

Undergraduates more frequently were trying to choose between going to graduate school immediately or going to work in a ghetto school system or poverty program. Although some expressed some guilt over opting for personal advancement through graduate school, they were able to rationalize this choice by asserting that they would be better equipped to serve the black community after receiving specialized training. Still a third group questioned their commitment to racial progress because they did not share this dilemma, but simply saw themselves as individuals who had the right to develop their potential in the direction that would be most profitable for them both personally and professionally. Pressures brought to bear on them by other more militant students led them to explore their motives with a therapist.

During this period, three black students suffered from psychotic breakdowns; all three dropped out of school and were eventually hospitalized. Five students made suicide attempts of varying degrees of severity, while one black female undergraduate did commit suicide. Seven students were granted medical leave for psychiatric reasons, but at least three of them were reenrolled by June of 1972. In three years eleven black students were infirmarized due to psychosomatic symptoms arising from their inability to cope with personal, social, or academic stresses.

Other complaints that were presented by ten percent or fewer of the black users were concerns about homosexuality, suicidal thoughts or preoccupations, the use or abuse of drugs and alcohol, and the inability to control aggression or other antisocial impulses. The handling of sexual and aggressive feelings was a salient issue, particularly among black males reared in the ghetto, where the overt expression of sexuality and aggression is tolerated as part of the life-style. Since the expression of these drives was soon found to be unacceptable on campus, these males did not find reinforcement for the hustling roles into which lower-class ghetto males are often socialized, for example, the street-corner dude, the playboy stud, or the cool cat. However, they were often subtly encouraged to adopt other roles, such as the black jock or the black militant, both of which engendered ambivalence in the campus community and were often perceived as stereotyped roles thrust upon blacks who had difficulty coping with more traditional college roles.

Duration and Termination Patterns

The average number of visits for black clinic users was 4.7 sessions. Graduate users tended to stay in treatment longer than undergraduate users, while female users had more sessions than male users. While students tended to stay in treatment longer with black therapists than with whites, the difference was not statistically significant.

There were different patterns of termination among the undergraduates and graduate student users. Among the undergraduates, 57.9 percent terminated therapy by mutual agreement with the therapist; 23.7 percent terminated due to a broken appointment or failure to make a follow-up appointment; 11.8 percent terminated because of withdrawal from school or hospitalization; and 6.5 percent terminated due to transfer to another resource. However, black graduate users terminated primarily for two reasons: 67 percent by mutual agreement with the therapist and 25 percent due to a broken appointment or failure to follow up. Only two students left school or transferred in the midst of ongoing therapy. Moreover, the graduate users tended to experiment with several therapists, while undergraduate users were more likely to remain with their initial contact.

Analysis of Clinic Utilization Data

These utilization statistics raise some significant issues regarding the mode and effectiveness of the treatment available to black students and to their ability to engage in the therapeutic process in this specific setting. First, utilization rates of black students showed a downward trend during this three-year period while their proportion increased in the general student body, and as the trend among the general student population showed increased rates. This downward trend may reflect several concomitant developments during this period: the increase in supportive services and counseling resources for minority students, the increase in social and cultural activities for black students, and the changing emphasis among students toward constructive rather than confrontational activities. All of these developments presumably created a more supportive environment for black students and reduced the causes for their emotional stress. Another equally plausible explanation is the possibility that the service was structured in too formal a manner, stressing appointments and contracts for a specific period of therapy, and that black students from working- and lower-class backgrounds, who accounted for much of the increase in black enrollment, did not find this compatible with their preference for crisis-oriented drop-in facilities. There was also in this group a traditional distrust of psychiatric services, and a lack of familiarity with preventive mental-health programs, thus an unwillingness to explore their emotional concerns in this manner.

Second, the decline in utilization rates according to class standing among black undergraduates presented a contrast to the general clinic population. One explanation for this difference may be that black undergraduates are more anxious than whites during their first year due to academic deficiencies and sociocultural differences, but that this anxiety and resulting emotional stress declines gradually in the following two years, with a slight increase again in the senior year because of concern over graduate school, career choice, or marital plans. The fact that four-fifths of the cases include concerns about academic competition and/or cultural and ethnic issues tends to substantiate this viewpoint; thus, by the end of the sophomore year many black students seem to have resolved these issues, and may be less likely to seek therapy for other types of problems in their last two years. Moreover, as they became acclimated, they may have obtained counseling from several other sources on campus where it is not necessary to define oneself as "emotionally troubled" to receive help.

Third, the duration of therapy was sometimes not consonant with the severity of the presenting symptoms or to the diagnosis. There may have been some problems of mutual communication between students and therapists, particularly because blacks do not like to expose their vulnerabilities to whites in positions of power. However, when a black student comes for help, the therapist may reasonably assume that he feels unable to cope with his usual tasks, and that he is probably in the midst of a crisis; thus it is incumbent upon the therapist to structure the therapeutic process as flexibly as possible so that the student will feel free to discuss his problems openly. Several studies have previously suggested that black students are more responsive to active interviewing techniques, more involvement by the therapist in the relationship, and specific behavior prescriptions to promote change. Black students also tend to respond more favorably to assistance with environmental changes that involve dealing with the college bureaucracy, such as changing a dormitory assignment, obtaining speech therapy, or resolving an academic crisis.

Since the proportion of black students who terminated by broken or canceled appointments or no returns was highest among the working- and lower-class students, and the proportion who terminated by mutual agreement was highest among upper and upper-middle class students, it is reasonable to assume that cultural differences and/or misconceptions about the therapeutic process adversely affected the ability of lower-class black students to engage in therapy with middle-class therapists. Thus, the socioeconomic status of a black student is positively related to the duration of therapy and the method of termination, that is, students from middle-class families tended to stay in therapy for longer periods and to terminate by mutual agreement with the therapist more frequently than those from nonmiddle-class backgrounds. This may indicate that the middle-class black student, like his white counterpart, is more knowledgeable and responsive to the therapeutic process, as well as the fact that middle-class therapists are more comfortable with patients who share their background and values; therefore there is little or no communication or cultural gap to impede the relationship. Conversely, lower-class students may perceive the structured semi-authoritarian therapeutic relationship as an extension of their frequently negative relationships with social workers, policemen, and other adult authority figures. Simply because these possibilities of misinterpretation do exist between black patients and white thera- pists, it is beneficial for the therapist to raise the racial issue very early in treatment in order to encourage a full discussion of the mutual feelings of ambivalence and prejudice that must be dealt with overtly or covertly during the relationship.

The problems experienced by black students are quite similar to the problems of white students, for instance, the usual emotional disorders and issues associated with late adolescence in our society. However, these similarities should not be allowed to obscure the differences in content and scope of these problems for black students, particularly in the area of racial-identity conflicts, interpersonal relations, and academic anxiety. Many of the symptoms experienced and the defense mechanisms exhibited by black students are directly related to their membership in a disadvantaged minority group that has developed its own subcultural style of language, dress, interpersonal behavior patterns, leisure interests, and values, as have been delineated by a wide range of social scientists.

Although these coping devices are sometimes dysfunctional, they have often developed in response to the prejudice and segregation imposed on blacks by the majority in society, so that it is predictable that black students will bring some of these behavior patterns to the therapeutic or counseling encounter. If their problems are viewed simply as normative adolescent conflicts, the therapist will perhaps miss the opportunity to help the student to deal with more basic feelings of inferiority, worthlessness, hostility, anger, and fear, all of which impede his development as a person and negatively affect his studies and his interpersonal relationships. In order to develop his full potential, a black student has to learn to cope with his marginal identity in a predominantly white milieu and to channel whatever negative feelings he may have into constructive channels. He can do this much more effectively if these feelings are acknowledged by counselors, administrators, and faculty members, who can then work cooperatively to provide opportunities for the student's growth and development.

Studies by Ellis (4), MacKey (11), Hammond (9), Davis and Swartz (3), and Gibbs (5), all tend to support the findings of the Stanford utilization survey with respect to the types of problems black students experience in integrated colleges, their patterns of using counseling and psychological services, and their attitudes toward the counsel- ing process and therapeutic relationship.

Patterns of Adaptation among Black Students
and Prospects for the Future

Pettigrew has pointed out that American blacks have developed three major modes of handling the oppressions or perceived oppression of the dominant majority group: movement toward the oppressor, movement away from the oppressor, and movement against the oppressor (12). As he conceptualizes these modes, blacks who *move toward* whites desire integration into the mainstream of American society; blacks who *move away from* whites wish to withdraw from contact with the dominant society; and blacks who *move against* whites express their hostility through aggressive actions aimed at white individuals or institutions.

In a study of the patterns of adaptation of black students at Stanford University, I identified these three patterns and an additional pattern of *movement with* the dominant culture (7). The four patterns were labeled as follows: the mode of *affirmation*, that is, movement with the dominant culture that involves an acceptance of one's ethnic identity while simultaneously relating to the relevant aspects of the dominant culture; the mode of *assimilation*, that is, movement toward the dominant culture that involves a rejection of one's own ethnicity and a total identification with the majority group; the mode of *separation*, that is, movement against the dominant culture that involves voluntary racial segregation and an aggressive rejection of the dominant group; and, finally, the mode of *withdrawal*, that is, movement away from the dominant culture, which involves isolation and a passive rejection of the dominant group. Although these four modes were identified in the context of a clinical study, it seems clear that they are the major modes of response employed by black students on white campuses, whether or not these students seek counseling for their problems.

How can black students maximize their experiences in predominantly white colleges and universities? As I have suggested elsewhere, the burden of improving the relationships between the students and the institutions falls on both groups; blame cannot be attributed to only one group, nor can change be expected of only one group in order for a new equilibrium to be established in the future.

There will continue to be ethnic tensions in the foreseeable future, so that blacks will continue to be perceived as a minority and treated in a somewhat different manner. However, the challenge for the students and the universities is learning to adapt to each other for the mutual growth and vitality of both constituencies.

References

1. Boyd, Harold. 1973. "Stanford Black Student Orientation Program." Mimeographed. Stanford University, California, September.
2. Coles, Robert. 1970. "Students Who Say No: Blacks, Radicals, Hippies." *International Psychiatry Clinic* 7:3-14.
3. Davis, Kenneth, and Swartz, Jacqueline. 1972. "Increasing Black Students' Utilization of Mental Health Services." *American Journal of Orthopsychiatry* 42:771-76.
4. Ellis, William. 1974. "The Preliminary Study of Black Student Utilization of Mental Health Services at the Division of Mental Hygiene, Yale University." Paper delivered at the Annual Meeting of the American Orthopsychiatric Association in San Francisco, April.
5. Gibbs, Jewelle T. 1970. "Black Students at a White University: An Exploratory Study." Master's research project. School of Social Welfare, University of California at Berkeley.
6. Gibbs, Jewelle T. 1973. "Black Students/White University: Different Expectations." *Personnel and Guidance Journal* 51 (March):463-69.
7. Gibbs, Jewelle T. 1974. "Patterns of Adaptation among Black Students at a Predominantly White University: Selected Case Studies." *American Journal of Orthopsychiatry* 44, no. 5 (October).
8. Gibbs, Jewelle T. 1975. "Use of Mental Health Services by Black Students at a Predominantly White University: A Three-Year Study." *American Journal of Orthopsychiatry* 45, no. 3 (April).
9. Hammond, C. 1970. "Paranoia and Prejudice: Recognition and Management of the Student from a Deprived Background." *International Psychiatry Clinic* 7:35-48.
10. Kilson, Martin. 1973. "Blacks at Harvard: Crisis and Change." *Harvard Bulletin*, April.
11. Mackey, Elvin. 1972. "Some Observations on Coping Styles of Black Students on White Campuses." *Journal of the American College Health Association* 21:126-30.
12. Pettigrew, Thomas. 1964. *A Profile of the Negro American.* New York: Van Nostrand.
13. Williams, Eddie, Jr. 1973. "Professor Kilson's Contentions: A Reply." *Harvard Bulletin*, June.

3

A Vision of Despair by
an Angry Black Writer:
John Williams
and *The Man Who Cried I Am*

David Owens

Max Reddick, the hero of John Williams's *The Man Who Cried I Am*, wants to complete the title by adding "a man," but his alter ego, Saminone (Sam-in-one), assures him that he is "a stone blackass nigger." In the novel Max lives for about thirty-six hours in the present, and during that time he relives his past life in an attempt to decide whether he is man or nigger. The conclusion he reaches, which is also the conclusion of the novel itself, is a sad one: rather than allow him to be a man, the white world will kill him and his kind in a complete holocaust of genocide. But even before the end Max knows he is already as good as dead, that the killing has been going on all of his life. At the core, then, this novel is the story of a lynching that took better than forty years to accomplish, but accomplished it was.

The aim of the white lynchers is the usual one: the victim's castration. It is quite obvious, therefore, that the emasculated Max Reddick has some important literary ancestors, one of whom is Jake Barnes in Hemingway's *The Sun also Rises*. But a comparison of the two shows fewer similarities than differences. The differences, however, are more important in illuminating Williams's basic attitudes toward the lynchers and the world in which both he and they must live. Barnes, like Reddick, knew all about the blackness of things in his emasculated state and was constantly seeking the light, but

there was no light; there was only horror. Hemingway's novel
suggests a way of handling the horror through an awareness of
irony and pity from which a stoic code emerges. Williams, however,
rejects Hemingway's elaborate metaphor of the bullring that Barnes
explains to Brett as a way of knowing what tragedy is and therefore
accepting it and living with it. There is no acceptance, no stoic
code, in *The Man Who Cried I Am*, for Max Reddick's story is one of
anger, the genesis of which is pity, whether given or received.

Williams has set himself the almost impossible task of maintaining
a tone of intense anger for some four hundred pages, the kind of
anger a civilized man feels in contemplating the metaphor of white
society as a lynching party. At the Cross it is likely there was no
pity; for pity would have been presumptuous; there was only the
tragic dialectic of anger and guilt. Williams elaborates this dialectic
by taking Max Reddick through a series of encounters with women,
nearly all of them white, who succeed in converting his sexual passion
into an ever-mounting anger, the anger of a man who realizes he is
being emasculated as he performs the act of love. His name then has
symbolic overtones: he is the "red dick," the burning, bloody
"red dick," the lyncher's victim.

A commentary on the narrative is given in a fantasy sequence at
the beginning of the novel. Max has gone to vent his anger on his
white ex-wife, Margrit, a Dutch woman. He means to tell her that
she was never more to him than a bleached version of a black girl,
Lillian Patch, with whom he was really in love and whose death
twenty years before he blames on the whites. In the fantasy Margrit,
as she drifts by on a conveyer belt, is trying out various kinds of
lighted filter cigarettes in her vagina. The image refers to Max, the
red dick, and it also refers to the transfer of the penis from Max to
Margrit. In the same fantasy, Max is being anally raped by Margrit
as she penetrates him with a cobalt machine. This part of the sequence
is pertinent because Max is dying of cancer of the rectum and has to
wear a cotton pad. The transfer is complete; he had been thoroughly
emasculated. Margrit is the last of a long line of white women with
whom he has slept. The lynch mob is led by white women.

As Max relives his experiences with white women, he comes to the
realization that he has been used by them as therapy for their
psychological frustrations. The realization that they had copulated
with him because they were mentally and spiritually sick makes his
pity for them turn to anger. He knows he has been had; he has been
the exploited one—a kind of male whore performing good deeds.
Exploitation of the black man by frustrated white women is funda-

mental to his realization that in the white world the only possible emotion for the black is anger, the kind that the lynch victim must feel, total annihilating frustration. He had been lynched in performing the act of love. The whites might as well go the whole way to genocide, which is their plan for settling the race question; and that is the philosophy with which the book ends.

Williams generalizes when he has Max say that he knows of no black who has not slept with a white woman. The irony the reader sees is that not only is the black man emasculated by white women but that he also will be destroyed by emasculated white men. The symbolic structure of the novel is completed when one of the white women, Regina, comes to Max when she is two-months pregnant by her white husband and asks him to sleep with her so that her child may have the strength of the protein in black semen.

There is a still larger context of the novel. At the beginning of the story, Max, whose vocation is writer-newspaper reporter, interviews a black, Boatwright, convicted of and sentenced to death for murdering a white man. At twenty-two, Boatwright had been the most brilliant graduate student in philosophy at Harvard, but he came to realize that there was no place for him in the white intellectual world. His act of rebellion was to kill a white man and then to cook and eat his heart and genitals. Here is both a reverse lynching and an attempt through cannibalism to get the strength of the victim. But even as a symbolic gesture it is neither dramatic nor horrible enough. Later in the novel Max recognizes that after the white crematoriums in white Germany and the atom bomb on Japan, Boatwright's act was too weak to reach men's minds and hearts. In a world habituated to horror, even cannibalism is tame, almost insipid; somehow the modern white world has not got as far as savagery. When Buchenwald and Hiroshima no longer are shocking, "what sort of violence is available to a novelist who would make his social protest?" is the question Williams is asking. His answer is, "genocide for the blacks." Man lives in a world that would have made Hobbes tremble; civilization is a schizophrenic fantasy; the reality is worse than barbarian. Max comes to see that Boatwright's act was a mere news item and to realize that he had pitied Boatwright for the futility of his rebellion, and suddenly he knows that his real feeling toward Boatwright was anger.

Williams consistently rules out pity as a possible emotion in our time. He turns then to questioning whether love may not be possible. The main story line is pitched to a search for identity as a *human being* through the act of love, but this, too, fails. The heart has lost touch with the genitals and the notion of identity is shattered.

The novel thus becomes a long death story whose main ingredient is the pain of incurable cancer and its paraphernalia of morphine, syringes, cobalt, knives, and the whiteness of pain. Max says of the hospital: "the whiteness, the purity of white did it. It made him want to scatter some dirty old semen all over it, the whiteness, make it more human." The nurses, the doctors, and the whole staff are white and dressed in white. But even in their best efforts to save life, they are not human. There is an ominous quality about them. "Gently they held his arm, pushed the needle into the big vein, and slipped in the sodium pentothal. Max went over the precipice," and they cut part of him away. The needle and the syringe image reappears at the end of the novel, for Max is killed with a hypodermic needle in the hand of a black C.I.A. agent working for the white rulers of society. He is killed because he is carrying papers containing a detailed, official plan for mass murder of blacks. The papers he carried had been willed to him by his friend Harry Ames, a black writer, who had been murdered a few days before by the same C.I.A. agent, a black turned white. It is clear, then, that Williams is suggesting that the crematoriums and the atom bombs have turned the white hospitals into a preview of genocide. Small wonder that he yearns to have black semen dirty them up and make them human.

Twenty years before, Max had been seduced by Ames's white wife who pleaded with him to make love to her "in friendship." All through the novel the black man is the instrument of mere sexual energy. To put this into the form of friendship is one of Williams's bitterest comments on a white-dominated society. The novel is about a black, but even more pointedly it is about a sick, decadent, emasculated white society that forces the black to be a mere penis; but the black knows that he is better than his white creators. He sees them for what they are: bleached bones in a dry land. They are being told by Williams that their white prophet, T. S. Eliot, was right: they have made a wasteland of their world; they are the hollow men, and their whiteness has all the terror-evoking strength that Melville had lined out for them a hundred years ago. But the terror has the force of tropism and this compounds it. It corrupts blacks.

On the same page as the description of the hospital there is what seems to be a key thematic statement of the matrix in which Williams sees Max's agony.

He was depressed. People whittling gleefully away at your flesh. Did they flush it away to join the shit and cloudy condoms floating in the rivers? Did fish nibble at it, a delicacy? *Look, man, here's a piece of Max Reddick! Have a taste!* Just what did they do with the flesh? It was a little bit of dying, already, *faster.* Even with their clean sheets, drugs, voluptuous nurses, flowers, diets, stainless steel tools, you were dying. But you knew that—piece of flesh, massed calcium, hunk of gristle, haphazard bit of matter, product of warm, ancient seas, still steaming lands wracked by unimaginable diastrophisms; the dark, dark, memories of that time (and the puzzle—reptile and fowl related—love them birds, have snake fever???) contained where, in the blood, the very atoms of the bone? Why remember more than most the vast laboring distance so filled with internecine horror and commonplace death, the gift of that raving bitch, evolution, nature, now made gentle with the title, Mother, and keep crying I Am?

Within this context, to keep crying "I am human" is futile, but man must maintain his humanity in spite of the bitchiness of nature. When whites and blacks lose their human ideals, when they cease to believe in human values even though these are illusions from a naturalistic point of view, then the great bitch has her way. Williams is echoing Henry Adams: somehow man has to get to Chartres to transform the bitch into the human mother, but how can he go when it's the bitch he believes in?

Ha! So your mother don't wear no drawers. How's that? Youse a motherfuckin' motherfucker, Oedipus Rex. Thass how come you knows so much.
I know so much because I'm your daddy.
Lissen to old king crap.
I am. I am a king.
Youse an ass. This ain't nuthin'; this ain't shit and needer is you.
I Am, I told you, damn it, I Am.

The natural man as distinguished from the human man is caught in the psychological trap of cannibalism and incest; he is a motherfucker who feeds on his brothers. Of such is Saminone's identity. It is no wonder that Williams never lets his readers forget the cancer whose psychological counterpart was elaborately set forth by Freud. For that, too, there is no known therapy as Williams sees it, except the illusions that Freud seemingly rejected.

But Max Reddick once had gone to the Chartres of the spirit.

It was with Lillian Patch. With her he knew what love is and came to see "that narrow place between what was real and what was not was the best place after all." But he also comes to see that the white world kills the Lillian Patches and love. Here is the big question the novel raises:

> They have killed both of us. God, Lillian, I'm mad. I am so mad, baby, and sorry for them, for me, for you. How did we get down here? We should have been out of here by now. Are we going to have to explode out?

There is no "narrow place" for the Max Reddicks nor his white lynchers. The novel tells the story of a society based on an elaborate psychological lynch law; it cannot be said that it is civilized; it is the tragic story of how it is since we have all become worse than the barbarians.

4

Black Liberation
and
Women's Lib

Linda J. M. LaRue

There is always a market for a movement. For Women's Liberation, the market will see to it that, in great quantity and unceasing redundancy, the message of "liberation" gets pushed in a way that women want to hear it, see it, and believe it. The market will appeal to their early consciousness with daring historical heroines, myths of great women in crisis, valid and half-baked truths about women's separatism and a new society, deeds or self-defense against exploitation, and words and words—pasted, paraded, and published so often that they reel, as tired old truths will, pounding the walls of that early consciousness until there is a rip or tear and the beginning of "sobering." And well it should be; it is necessary—it is also familiar.

It was barely twenty historical minutes ago that blacks first celebrated their new consciousness with the palm wine of self-appreciation and the pursuit of liberation. We, too, sang of our fine dark heroes, sported our elaborate dashikis, passed both half-baked and valid tales of our virtues among ourselves, and made corporations like Johnson and Company not uncomfortably rich from their sale of "Afrosheen." And well it was; it was necessary—but it was both unfamiliar and painful.

This essay will speak to the sobering moments in both movements as a new crisis imperceptibly creeps up on an entity who is both black and a woman. To date, little synthesis has been proposed between the problems of the liberation of women and that of blacks. Indeed, it seems that just when Eldridge Cleaver's tribute, "To All Black Women from All Black Men," had at least anesthetized the psychic degradation of mutual disdain and distrust existing between black men and black women, there emerged a new movement to reincense black women against black men and reopen the old wounds with salty agitation. Women's Liberation has and will affect black liberation. The question is how.

At this time, there is little need to enumerate what will eventually come to be the clichés of women's "oppression" throughout the ages. As for accentuation and denunciation of past injustices, allow the women in the first stages of consciousness to write that commentary. They will be much more diligent in researching "oppression's" sordid details. It suffices to say, as Gordon Allport pointed out, "For some people. . .women are viewed as a wholly different species from men, usually an inferior species. Such primary and secondary sex differences as exist, are greatly exaggerated and are inflated into imaginary distinctions that justify discrimination."

What Is Bad about It?

First to be discussed is what the movement literature calls the *common oppression* of blacks and women. This is a tasty abstraction designed purposely or inadvertently to give validity and seriousness to the women's movement through an appeal to universality of plight. Every movement worth its revolutionary salt makes these headliner generalities about common oppression with others. However, let it be stated unequivocally that the American white woman has had a better opportunity to live a free and fulfilling life, both mentally and physically, than any other group in the United States, excluding her white husband. Thus, any attempt to analogize black oppression with the plight of the American white woman has all the validity of comparing the neck of a hanging man with the rope-burned hands of an amateur mountain climber.

"Common oppression" is fine for rhetoric, but it does not reflect the actual distance between the oppression of the black man and woman who are unemployed and the "oppression" of the American white woman who is "sick and tired" of *Playboy* foldouts, of Christian Dior lowering hemlines or adding ruffles, or of Miss Clairol telling her that blondes have more fun. What does the black woman on welfare who has difficulty feeding her children have in common with the discontent of the suburban mother who has the luxury to protest washing the dishes on which her family's full meal was consumed?

The surge of "common oppression" rhetoric and propaganda may lure the unsuspecting into an intellectual alliance with the goals of Women's Liberation, but this is not a wise alliance. The problem is not that women do not need to be liberated from the shackles of their present unfulfillment, but rather that the depth, the extent, the intensity, the importance, indeed the suffering and depravity of the real oppression blacks have experienced can only be minimized in an alliance with women who have heretofore suffered little more than boredom, gentle repression, and dishpan hands.

This disproportion of urgency and need can be seen in a hundred examples. It is a fact that when white women received their voting rights most blacks—male and female—were systematically disenfranchised and had been that way since after Reconstruction. And even in 1970, when women's right of franchise is rarely questioned, it is still less than common for blacks to vote in some areas of the South. Or take the tastelessly joined plight of oppressed middle-class and poor women in the matter of abortion. Actual circumstances boil down to this: middle-class women decide when it is convenient to have children, while poor women decide the prudence of bringing into a world of already scarce resources another mouth to feed. Neither their motives nor their projects are the same. But current literature leads one to lump the decisions of these two women under one generalization, when in fact the difference between the plights of these two women is as clear as the difference between being hungry and out of work, compared with skipping lunch and taking the day off.

Recently, Women's Lib advocates demanded that a local women's magazine be "manned" by a woman editor. Other segments of the women's movement have carried on similar campaigns in industry and business. But if white women have heretofore remained silent while white men maintained the better positions and monopolized the opportunities by excluding blacks, can we really expect that white women, when put in direct competition for employment, will be any more open-minded than their male counterparts when it comes to the hiring of black males and females in the same positions for which they are competing? American history is not very reassuring that white females will be any less tempted than their husbands to take advantage of the fact that they are white in an economy that favors whites.

In short, one can argue that Women's Liberation has not only attached itself to the black movement but has done so with only marginal concern for black women and black liberation and functional concern for the rights of white women. It is entirely possible that Women's Liberation has developed a sudden attachment to the black-liberation movement as a ploy to share the attention that it has taken blacks 400 years to generate. Max Weber speaks of this parasitic relationship:

> If the participants expect the admission of others will lead to an improvement of their situation, an improvement in degree, in kind, in the security or the value of the satisfaction, their interest will be in keeping the relationship open. . . .
>
> The principal motives for closure of a relationship are, a) the maintenance of quality, which is often combined with the interest in prestige and the consequent opportunities to enjoy honor, and even profit, b) orientation to the scarcity of advantages in their bearing on consumption needs, and c) orientation to the scarcity of opportunities for acquisition.

The industrial demands of two world wars temporarily offset the racial limitations to mobility and allowed blacks to enter industry as an important labor force. Similarly, women have benefited from an expanded science and industrialization. With their biological limitations successfully brought under control by the pill and offset by automation, an impressively large and available labor force of women was created.

The black labor force, however, was never fully employed and has always represented a substantial percentage of the unemployed in the American economy. Presently, it may now be driven into greater unemployment as white women converge at every level on an already dwindling job market.

Ideally, Women's Liberation was considered a promising beginning of the "oppressed rising everywhere" in the typically Marxian fashion to which many blacks seem drawn. Instead, the specter of racism and inadequate education, job discrimination, and even greater unequal opportunity will become more than ever before a function of neither maleness nor femaleness, but blackness.

Moreover, though most radical, white Women's Lib advocates fail to realize the possibility, their liberation, if and when it comes, may spell a strengthening of other status-quo values from which they also seek liberation. As more and more women participate in the decision-making process through the movement, the few radical women in the "struggle" will be outnumbered by the more traditional middle-class women. This means that the traditional women will be in a position to take advantage of new opportunities that radical Women's Liberation has struggled to win. Voting studies now reflect that the traditional woman, middle class and above, tends to vote the same way as her husband. Blacks have dealt with these husbands in the effort to secure jobs, housing, and education; they know the unlikelihood of either blacks or radicals gaining significantly from the open mobility of less tolerant women whose viewpoints differ little from that of their husbands.

My concern at this historical moment [1970] is to prevent any unintelligent alliance of black people with white women in this new liberation movement. Rhetoric and anathema hurled at the right industrial complex, idealism that speaks of a final humanism, and denunciations of the system that makes competition a fact of life do not mean that Women's Liberation has as its goal anyone else's liberation except its own.

It is time that definitions be made clear. Blacks are oppressed— and that means unreasonably burdened, unjustly, severely, rigorously, cruelly, and harshly fettered by white authority. White women are only suppressed—and that means checked, restrained, excluded from conscious and overt activity. And there is a difference.

What Is Good about It?

The dangers of an unintelligent alliance with Women's Liberation will bring some to conclude that female suppression is the only way to protect against a new economic threat. For others, a broader answer is required, which will enable Women's Liberation to be seen in perspective.

If we are candid with ourselves, we must accept the fact that, despite our beloved rhetoric of Pan-Africanism, our vision of Third World liberation, and perhaps our dreams of a world state of multiracial humanism, most blacks still want the proverbial "piece of the cake." American values are difficult to discard, for, contrary to what the more militant "brothers" would have us believe, Americanism does not end with the adoption of Afro hairstyles on pregnant women covered in long African robes.

[...]

More to the point, for this essay, is the striking coincidence of the rebirth of liberation struggles in the sixties with a whole platform of "women's place" advocates who immediately relegated black women to home and babies.

[. . .]

The study of many developing areas reflects at least an attempt to allow freedom of education and opportunity to women. Yet black Americans have not adopted the developing areas' new role paradigm, but rather the Puritan-American status of "home and babies" advocated by the capitalist Muslims. This reflects either ingrained Americanism or the lack of the simplest imagination.

Still, to say that black women must be freed before the black movement can attain full revolutionary consciousness is meaningless because of its malleability. It makes much more sense to say that black women must be freed from the unsatisfactory male-female role relationship, which was adopted from whites as the paradigm of the good family, because it indicates the incompatibility of white role models with the goal of black liberation. If there is anything to be learned from the current Women's Liberation, it is that roles are not ascribed and inherent, but adopted and interchangeable in every respect—except pregnancy, breast feeding, and the system generally employed to bring the two former into existence.

Role integration, which will be proffered as the goal and the strength of the black family, is substantially different from the role "usurpation" of men by women, or vice versa. It points to what I see as an essential process of incorporation as equals, a permanent equality of merit, responsibility, and respect. The fact that the roles of man and woman are deemed in American society to be natural and divine leads to false ego attachments to these roles. During slavery and following Reconstruction, black men felt inferior for a great number of reasons, among them that they were unable to work in positions comparable to the ones to which black women were assigned. With these female positions often went fringe benefits of extra food, clothes, and perhaps elementary reading and writing skills. Black women were in turn jealous of white women and often felt inadequate and inferior because there was constantly paraded in front of them the white woman of luxury who had no need to work and who could, as Sojourner Truth pointed out, "be helped into carriages, and lifted over ditches, and. . .have the best place every-where."

Yet, despite (or, rather, because of) this history, black people have an obligation, as do white women, to recognize that the designation of "mother-head" or "father-head" does not imply inferiority of one and the superiority of the other. They are merely arbitrary role distinctions that vary from culture to culture and circumstance to circumstance.

Thus to quip, as it has been popularly done, that the only place in the black movement for black women is prone is actually supporting a white role ideal; and it is a compliment to neither men nor women to advocate such sexual capitalism or sexual colonialism.

[...]

Competition

Most, but not all, American relationships are based on some type of exclusive competition of the superior, and the exclusive competition of the inferior. This means essentially that the poor, the uneducated, the deprived, and the minorities compete among themselves for the same scarce resources and inferior opportunities. At the same time, the privileged, middle-class, educated, and select white minorities compete with each other for rather plentiful resources and superior opportunities for prestige and power. Competition between the two large groups is rare due to the fact that elements who qualify are almost invariably absorbed to some extent (note the black middle class) by the group to which they seek entry. It will be understood that in this situation there is only one equal relationship between man and woman—black and white—in America, and this equality is based on the ability to force one's way into qualifying for the same resources.

Instead of attempting to modify this competitive definition within the black movement, many black males have affirmed it as a way of maintaining the closure of male monopolization of scarce benefits and making the "dominion of males" impenetrable to black females. This is, of course, very much the American way of exploitation.

The order of logic that makes it possible to pronounce, as did Robert Staples, that "black women cannot be free qua women until all blacks attain their liberation" assumes that black women will be able to separate their femaleness from their blackness—and thus will be able to be free as blacks, if not free as women; or that male freedom ought to come first; or finally that the freedom of black people as a whole is not one and the same.

Only with the concept of role integration can we hope to rise above the petty demarcations of human freedom that America is noted for, and that are unfortunately inherent in Staples's remark. Role integration involves the realization of two things. The first of these is that ego attachments to particular activities or traits must be abolished as a method of determining malehood and femalehood. Instead, ego attachments must be distributed to a wider variety of tasks and traits in order to weaken the power of one activity in determining self-worth. And the second is the realization that the flexibility of a people in effecting role alternation and role integration has been a historically proven asset to the survival of any people.

The unwitting adoption and the knowing perpetuation by black people of the American sexual paradigm reflect three interrelated situations: a) black people's growing sense of security and well-being, and their failure to recognize the extent of black problems; b) black people's overidentification with the dominant group, even though the survival of blacks in America is not assured; and c) black people's belief in the myth of "matriarchy" and their subsequent rejection of role integration as unnatural and unnecessary.

While the rhetoric of black power and the advocates of cultural nationalism laud black people for their ability to struggle under oppressive odds, they simultaneously seek to strip away or incapacitate the phenomenon of role integration—the very means by which blacks were able to survive. They seek to replace it with an intractable role separation that would completely sap the strength of the black movement because it would inhibit the mobilization of both women and men. It was this ability to mobilize black men and women that guaranteed survival during slavery.

A Warmed-over Throne

The strength of role integration is sorely overlooked as blacks throw away the hot comb, the bleach cream, the lye—yet insist on maintaining the worst of American values by placing the strength of black women in the traction of the white female status. I should think that black men would want a better status for their sister black women—indeed, that black women would want a better status of themselves—than a warmed-over throne of women's inferiority, which some white women have so recently abandoned. If white radical thought has called upon the strength of all women to take a position of responsibility and power, can blacks afford to relegate black women to "home and babies"?

The cry of black women's liberation is a cry against chaining a very much-needed labor force and agitating force to a role that belongs to impotent, apolitical white women. Blacks speak lovingly of the vanguard and the importance of women in the struggle yet fail to recognize that women have been assigned a new place, based on the white-ascribed characteristics of women rather than on their actual potential. The black movement needs its women in a position of struggle, not prone. The struggle that blacks face is not taking place between knives and forks, at the washboard, or in the diaper pail. It is taking place on the labor market, at the polls, in government, in the protection of black communities, in local neighborhood power struggles, in housing, and in education. Can blacks afford to be so unobservant of current events as to send their women to fight a nonexistent battle in a dishpan?

Even now, the black adoption of white evaluations of women has begun to show its effects on black women in distinctive ways. The black-liberation movement has created a politicized, unliberated copy of white womanhood. Black women who participated in the struggle have failed to recognize, for the most part, the unique contradiction between their professed renunciation of capitalist competition and their acceptance of sexual colonialism. The failure of the black movement to resolve or even deal with this dilemma has perpetuated the following attitudes in politicized black women in America:

The belief in the myth of the matriarchy has made the black woman feel ashamed of her strength, and so to redeem herself she has adopted from whites the belief that superiority and dominance of the male are the most "natural" and "normal" relationships. She consequently believes that black women ought to be suppressed in order to attain that "natural balance."

Because the white woman's role has been held up as an example to all black women, many black women feel inadequate and so ardently compete in "femininity" with white females for black male's attention. They further compete with black females in an attempt to be the "blackest and most feminine," thereby superior to their fellow black sisters in appealing to politicized black men. They compete also with the apolitical black female in an attempt to keep black males from "regressing" back to females whom they feel had more "practice" in the traditional role of white women than they have had.

Finally, the black woman emphasizes the traditional role of

women, such as housekeeping, children, supportive roles, and self-maintenance, but she politicizes these roles by calling them the role of black women. She then adopts the attitude that her job and her life is to have more children who can be used in the vanguard of the black struggle.

Black women, as the song "Black Pearl" relates, have been put up where they belong—but by American standards. The birth of Women's Liberation is an opportunity for the black movement to come back to its senses. The black woman is demanding a new set of female definitions and a recognition of herself as a citizen, companion, and comrade, not a matriarchal villain or a stepstool baby maker. Role integration advocates the complementary recognition of man and woman, not the competitive recognition of same.

The recent unabated controversy over the use of birth control in the black community is of grave importance here. Black people, even the "most liberated of mind," are still infused with the ascribed inferiority of females and the natural superiority of males. These same values foster the idea of "good blood" in children. If, indeed, there can be any black liberation, it must start with the recognition of contradictions such as that involving black children.

It gives a great many black males pride to speak, as Robert Staples does, of the "role of the black woman in the black-liberation struggle [as] an important one [that] cannot be forgotten. From her womb have come the revolutionary warriors of our time."

Conceiving of Bastards

How many potential "revolutionary warriors" stand abandoned in orphanages while blacks rhetoricize disdain for birth control as a "trick of the Man" to half the growth of black population? Why are there not more revolutionary couples adopting black children? Could it be that the concept of bastard, which is equivalent to inferiority in our society, reflects black Anglo-Saxonism? Do blacks—like whites—discriminate against black babies because they do not represent "our own personal" image? Or do blacks, like the most racist of whites, require that a child be of their own blood before they can love that child or feed it? Does the vanguard, of which Dr. Staples so reverently speaks, recognize the existence of the term *bastard*?

Would it not be more revolutionary for blacks to advocate a five-year moratorium on black births until every black baby in the American orphanage was adopted by one or more black parents?

Then blacks would really have a valid reason for continuing to give birth. Children would mean more than simply a role for black women to play, or fuel for the legendary vanguard. Indeed, blacks would be able to tap the potential of the existing children and could sensibly add more potential to the black struggle for liberation. To do this would be to do something no other modern civilization has ever done, and blacks would be allowing every black child to have a home and not just a plot in some understaffed children's penal farm.

What makes a healthy black baby in an orphanage different from "our own flesh and blood"? Except for the value of inferiority-superiority, and the concept of "bastard" that accompanies it, there is nothing "wrong" with an orphaned child save what white society has taught us to perceive.

If we confine our reading to the literature of the Women's Liberation movement, it appears that women are just one more group in the march of the rising oppressed masses. If we see it as it is, however, Women's Liberation is a clear threat to an already dwindling job market. It is a threat to the economic well-being and progress of blacks and other minority groups. The few positions opening up in areas of power will be greeted with a surge of new applicants, which means that some women (I expect them to be generally white) will be hired in an effort to be "fair to all oppressed groups" or to be "an equal opportunity employer." Women's Liberation will probably end up having used the black movement as a stepping-stone to opportunities in a highly competitive economy. Women's Liberation represents another mouth to feed in a very stingy economy. In short, it will probably mean less for groups that are really oppressed, since distribution does not care who has been in the line the longest (and it is the squeaky hinge that gets the oil).

At the same time, however, Women's Liberation must be seen as a light in which blacks can rediscover their deeply ingrained American values. Had the crisis of Women's Liberation not emerged, we would never really have recognized the myth of matriarchy or the new assignment of black women to roles that radical white women are already vacating. Through Women's Liberation we can see how deeply indoctrinated many blacks are by the concept of inferiority. This is true to the extent that when speaking of their wives and children they have employed American values of their worth and American definitions of their meaning.

Most important, we can conclude that black women's liberation and black men's liberation is what we mean when we speak of the liberation of black people. The one cannot be mentioned without implying the other. Many suspect that Women's Liberation will enhance the distrust and dissension existing between black men and black women. I maintain that the true liberation of black people depends on their rejection of the inferiority of women, the rejection of competition as the only viable relationship between men and their reaffirmation of respect for man's general human potential in whatever form—man, child, or woman—it is conceived. If both men and women are liberated, then competition between the sexes no longer exists, and sexual exploitation becomes a remnant of social immaturity.

5

Ethnic Resentment

Fred Barbaro

The antipoverty and other Great Society programs were launched in a decade that was notable for its professed altruism. The proclaimed objective was the elimination of poverty and many of its by-products. By the time the decade came to a close the dream had tarnished in the wake of violence against political leaders, civil disorders, a prolonged war in Vietnam, and police violence directed against our youth.

Perhaps the results were predictable: as the blacks, the most visible minority, sought to hasten the conversion of the dream to reality, other groups waited for their opportunities to recoup real or imaginary losses sustained during the 1960s. It was not so easy to foretell, however, the apparent hostility of other minorities against blacks resulting from the implementation of the Kennedy-Johnson domestic programs. Blacks were increasingly seen as the major beneficiaries of these programs and quickly became the targets of other groups frustrated by their inability to receive what they perceived to be their fair share. As the war effort consumed more and more resources and the promised program expansion failed to reach the level where these groups could be served, antiblack sentiments increased. Nonblack minority groups reasoned that there would only be one pie, that it was being baked for and consumed by blacks, and that they must more aggressively stake their claims if they wished to receive a slice of that pie.

Antiblack sentiment was expressed in a variety of ways and with varying degrees of hostility:

A proposal for a fellowship program for Puerto Ricans emphasizes the educational gap between Puerto Ricans and blacks rather than with the white majority.

An agency's report on Jewish participation in the antipoverty program states that although officials in the program are not anti-Semitic, "they are unaware of Jewish poverty and. . .they are more interested in serving 'their own.' "

Mexican Americans, the largest minority group in Los Angeles, express resentment over the channeling of most of the public and private aid into the black community of Watts.

This interminority rivalry not only seems to have been a major deterrent to the development of a coalition to seek the incremental expansion of programs to meet common needs, but also contributed to the eradication of existing cooperative efforts among minorities. This same rivalry has led to an intensification of the tendency of each group to look inward and to make its claims upon the institutions of government in conflict with, and sometimes at the expense of, other organized interest groups.

These ethnic-group struggles are not unique in American politics. For example, the Irish and Italians competed for political advantage long before the blacks and Puerto Ricans arrived in New York City in any sizable number. Nor is there any evidence to suggest that Jews, Puerto Ricans, blacks, and Chicanos would behave differently from other groups under similar circumstances. However, the confluence of political and social circumstances in the sixties shaped a situation in which common aspirations and goals disintegrated in the crosscurrents of individual group demands. A review of the origin and nature of the conflict over limited program resources and the resulting tendency of each group to seek separatist solutions to its problems may be instructive as we seek clues to how these problems will be handled in the seventies.

Other groups such as the Polish Americans and Italian Americans were not included in this discussion because their relationship with blacks differed qualitatively from the relationships of groups previously mentioned. Members of the Italian and Polish communities have not participated in Great Society programs in large numbers and only recently have begun to reconsider that position. In addition to not wanting to associate with what they perceived to be black-oriented programs, they also knew that their participation would result in their neighborhoods being designated as poverty areas—a definition they were not willing to accept. For example, Italian Americans in Newark would not permit the establishment of a field office of the antipoverty agency in their ward, and thereby denied themselves thousands of dollars worth of program jobs and needed services. Finally, the intensity of the feelings between these groups and blacks, and their tendency to support conservative causes, does not make them likely candidates for a liberal coalition in the near future.

Black Preference: Fact or Fancy?

A common view expressed by most minority-group members interviewed was that the Kennedy-Johnson programs were designed for blacks, and, in fact, blacks did reap most of the benefits from the program. This conclusion is supported by the literature on the program written by members of the task force that drafted the original legislation, administered the program on the federal and local levels, or conducted studies of its operations.

At what point in time did the New Frontier-Great Society programs become black oriented? In *Regulating the Poor*, Piven and Cloward argue that from the start the programs were conceived and designed as a political strategy to buttress an obvious trend in Democratic presidential politics—the importance of the big-city vote. The migration of blacks to the North and the weakening of the North-South Democratic coalition, both of which began following World War II, led to the prominence of the cities in Democratic party strategy. Although Kennedy's victory was attributable to his performance in the cities, his margin of victory was small. The full potential of the cities was not yet realized.

Since local political parties were controlled by whites and few attempts to recruit and register blacks had been made, a means to tap the repository urban-black vote had to be found. The best method to nurture the black vote seemed to be the extension of municipal service to them while avoiding alienation of the urban-white vote. Thus, the antipoverty programs focused on the cities.

The consequent urban bias of antipoverty programs was documented by Sar Levitan. The ten largest recipients of Community Action Program (C.A.P.) funds, fiscal years 1965-68, were: New York City; Chicago; Los Angeles; Philadelphia; Detroit; St. Louis; Washington, D.C.; Boston; Atlanta; and Pittsburgh. Together they received almost three times the national average per person. "Illinois received

$39.4 million in CAP funds in fiscal 1967, while Alabama, with
almost the same number of poor people, received only $17.5 million;
New Jersey and Wisconsin, despite similar poverty populations, were
granted $26.4 million and $8.9 million, respectively." In addition to
the political need for the urban vote there were other reasons,
perhaps of equal importance. In such volatile and complex times as
the sixties, it is not hazardous to speculate that social policy was
the result of several demands made on the political system.

Among the most persistent demands being made at the time of the
1960 presidential election were the ones proposed by the black-
white coalition in the civil-rights movement. Although the initial
cry was for "freedom," suggesting civil-rights legislation as the
solution, by the time of the 1963 March on Washington, the slogan
included jobs, housing, and education as well as freedom.

A review of John F. Kennedy's personal life and early political
career would disclose little to suggest that he was prepared either
intellectually or emotionally to handle the direct-action stage of the
movement. As a legislator he did not require black votes to win
elections in Massachusetts nor did he sponsor any significant
legislation in the civil-rights area. Yet as a national candidate he
became increasingly aware of these issues. Presidential adviser
Theodore Sorensen stated, "Most Negro leaders were shrewd judges
of which politicians cared deeply about their values and which cared
chiefly about their votes—and while Kennedy may have initially
been more influenced by the second concern, by the 1960s, the first
had become more and more important to him."

Kennedy's references to poverty in America during his campaign
were not directed at alleviating black poverty nor is there evidence
that he envisioned an attack on poverty along the lines of the 1964
act. His rhetoric was a challenge to eight years of Republican
"prosperity," in spite of a six percent unemployment level. After
his election he turned to Walter Heller, chairman of the Council
of Economic Advisors, to direct his antipoverty strategy, which
resulted in attempts to stimulate the economy through tax deductions
and other devices. But by the spring of 1963 he realized that a
stimulated economy was not enough and instructed Heller to plan a
broad and comprehensive war against poverty.

After he became president, Lyndon Johnson endorsed Kennedy's
decision. He proceeded to skillfully engineer the passage of the
Economic Opportunity Act in 1964, the Civil Rights Bill of 1964, and
the Voting Rights Bill of 1965 as "living memorials" to President
Kennedy. By this time few doubted that the legislative package was

aimed at black America to relieve the pressure building up in the nation's streets. The president's "We Shall Overcome" speech before Congress was another attempt to lead and hopefully contain the pace of the movement. But Johnson was quickly running out of inexpensive measures, and although he knew that the present programs were inadequate, his sense that the country was not prepared for a bold new program to benefit blacks, prevented dramatic action. He needed time.

According to Lee Rainwater and William L. Yancey, it was Daniel P. Moynihan and Richard N. Goodwin, both holdovers from the Kennedy administration, who persuaded Johnson that more must be done to deal with black poverty. The result of their efforts was the White House Conference, "To Fulfill These Rights," a traditional device employed by several administrations to educate the public by focusing national attention on a problem, and to buy time. Johnson's decision to announce his plans for the conference at the federally financed, mostly black, Howard University, was significant. If there were any doubts before the speech regarding who would benefit from this new federal activity, there were none afterward. The speech, written by Goodwin and Moynihan, incorporated many of the conclusions of a report prepared by Moynihan entitled, *The Negro Family: The Case for National Action.* His thesis of the report was that "freedom was not enough" and he then proceeded to document the "widening gulf" between black and white citizens. Moynihan's solutions were expensive, for example, a full-employment program for males and a guaranteed annual income, and the conference was designed to work out the details and to gather support for the programs.

In August 1965, Watts erupted and white America felt betrayed. The controversy over the "Moynihan Report" destroyed the White House Conference. The deepening involvement in Vietnam made it impossible to have both "guns and butter." Johnson did not follow up on the bold promises he made at Howard University and instead proposed the modest Model Cities program.

The motivation and the initiative taken by the executive branch in responding to black demands are clear: first political then social pressure shaped policy. Legislative intent is not always realized during the implementation stage, however. What factors led to the favored status of blacks in dispersal of funds? Sar Levitan's study, previously cited to indicate the urban bias of the programs, concludes that blacks received a far greater share of the benefits from these programs than their percentage in the poor population would warrant.

Levitan supports this statement by his analysis of ethnic census data gathered on various components of the program by the Office of Economic Opportunity (O.E.O.), the Department of Labor, and the Bureau of the Census.

Levitan attributes the black advantage to factors related to the civil-rights movement. "With almost every community eligible for CAP dollars, distribution of funds on the basis of poverty population was virtually impossible. . . .The only explanation. . .is that areas with the most effective organization and sophistication in the art of grantmanship received the largest proportion of funds. 'Rural discrimination' was closely related to the absence of effective local organization in sparsely populated rural areas." Levitan argues that the movement "gave the Negro. . .an organizational base which was lacking among whites who were poor."

The author agrees that the civil-rights experience provided blacks with a distinct advantage over other groups who lacked an organizational base on the local level, and that the antipoverty program became interwoven in the battle for black equality. But the political and social pressures on the policymakers described above seem to contradict Levitan's contention that "those who drafted the Economic Opportunity Act in 1964 were unaware that they were drafting a civil-rights law." It was the whites who were involved in the task force, supported the legislation, helped draw up guidelines, administered the program, and sat on the boards of the Community Action Agencies (C.A.A.) who were responsible for the black bias of the program. Many had been associated with liberal causes for years and moved into antipoverty jobs because, as Levitan states, "it was possible to view the early OEO as a potential institutional base for the second phase of the civil-rights movement." Later, in addition to battling Puerto Ricans and Chicanos for program resources, blacks would compete with these same whites for top administrative jobs and control over "their" program.

With this overview of the antipoverty program's inception and development, it will be usedful to examine the history of three minority groups who sought to share in the benefits of the programs and found themselves embroiled in interminority disputes.

The Puerto Rican Case

To the unsophisticated observer, reports of black-Puerto Rican conflict are likely to be greeted with surprise. From the earliest days of the civil-rights movement the groups have been linked together in an apparently solid coalition. However, for those people involved and who monitored the scene closely, the cry for "jobs for blacks and Puerto Ricans" was more of a strategic device than a factual description of the true nature of the relationship between the groups. Puerto Rican participation in civil-rights organizations and on picket lines was lower than for whites. If they did participate, they were not likely to hold leadership positions and, equally important, were not representative of the larger Puerto Rican community.

Puerto Rican leaders began seeking other arrangements to advance their cause even before the replacement of the civil-rights movement with Black Power organizations. They reasoned that their participation resulted in minimal rewards and a submergence of their identity and special problems. They lacked an organizational base in local communities, and had hardly any professional organizations exclusively concerned about their problems. If they did participate in a protest action and were successful in developing twenty-five jobs for minority workers, for example, they had some difficulty in producing qualified applicants, while the local Urban League could produce twice that number in twenty-four hours.

It was not easy for the Puerto Rican leadership to break away. They were charged with racism and a desire not to associate with blacks because they ranked low on the socioeconomic ladder. There was some truth to this charge among the rank and file whose cultural background and disparate life experiences made it difficult for them to identify with black aspirations. By and large it was not true of the leadership. Regardless of how well they articulated their predicament, few provided them with a sympathetic hearing. Americans who cared at all focused on black-white relations. Puerto Ricans began looking inward for their solutions.

For the Puerto Rican leadership it became a problem of attracting the nation's attention. All special interest groups face this task, and of course the fewer people affected, the more difficult it is to interest the media, legislators, and the populace. After all, what does the average American know about Puerto Rico or Puerto Ricans? Puerto Rico is a vacation paradise that is somehow related politically to this country. Were Puerto Ricans not involved in shootings directed against President Truman and members of Congress? Puerto Rican teenage gangs "rumbled" with other gangs in the 1950s. What ever happened to them? Puerto Ricans now want jobs and freedom. Every bit of knowledge was accompanied by a boat load of questions attesting to the nation's general ignorance on the subject.

Faced with this dilemma, Puerto Ricans, so accustomed to submerging black-Puerto Rican differences under the "freedom umbrella," began to emphasize their differences. Blacks already had the nation's attention and coattailing in this manner had greater potential than under the previous arrangement. Statistical evidence was presented to show that Puerto Ricans were lagging behind both blacks and whites in many areas. Soon whites were dropped from the comparison. The motivation was, as one spokesman put it, "to change the impression held by most people that because many of us are white, we are making it. This evidence should dispel that notion."

Statistics were always cited in terms of percentages, for 1.5 million Puerto Ricans (the Puerto Ricans actually claim three million mainland residents) could not build as strong a case when speaking in terms of absolute numbers. With twenty-two million to draw from, blacks could match numbers with other minority groups in the areas of poverty and its related miseries. But these kinds of arguments were pointless when one considered the fact that the funds were not adequate to even begin to meet the needs of any group. In addition, blacks could always add other variables like "justice" to bolster their claim for preferential treatment. Puerto Ricans, Chicanos, and Jews could add their special grievances and the spiral would continue to climb but the main problem of insufficient funds would remain. Under these conditions equitable allocations were difficult, if not impossible.

In New York City, where almost one million Puerto Ricans live, the leadership joined the blacks in seeking a decentralized program. Few trusted City Hall to cater to their interests; in fact, one of the unique features of the act was that it was possible to bypass both the state and local governments. In retrospect, some among the leaders feel that decentralization was a mistake. Twenty-six local community corporations were established, controlled mostly by blacks, while Puerto Ricans received funds for twelve citywide programs. This arrangement was based in part on the related beliefs that Puerto Ricans who lived in the designated poverty areas would receive services and that Puerto Ricans were dispersed throughout the city and needed citywide programs to serve them. It was not long before both beliefs were challenged.

In 1967, a study that monitored Puerto Rican residential patterns dispelled the notion that Puerto Ricans were leaving their ghettos and were moving to new locations throughout the city. "Almost without exception," the *New York Times* found, "Puerto Rican settlements appear as foothills to Negro areas." As neighbors they began a fierce competition for control of the community corporations and their jobs and services. A winner-takes-all psychology soon developed and during the early days of the program, only the blacks were well organized enough to "take."

At the local level there was little patience with people who lectured on power politics or the "big picture." Puerto Ricans could understand that white suburbanites ran the banks and corporations, but Puerto Ricans did not have access to that action. As they saw it, the blacks were the "haves" and they were the "have nots." Attempts to negotiate a larger percentage of the funds for Puerto Rican programs were frustrated at every turn. For example, in Newark Puerto Ricans fought for three years to get their only proposal for a $30,000 program approved by the local CAA, which was allocated for more than five million dollars for programs. They picketed meetings of the board of directors and staged several "sit-ins" at the CAA headquarters. Finally, during a heated debate, a young Puerto Rican shouted, "do we have to riot to get funds?" After several confrontations along these lines relationships between the groups were frozen at a civil, but less than cordial, level.

Black administrators were not unsympathetic but they had problems of their own. Their constituencies felt that black protest was responsible for the enabling legislation and that they were therefore entitled to its benefits. The funds available did not begin to meet the needs of the black community in terms of services or jobs. Of equal importance was the fact that after the original programs were funded, allocations to many of the CAAs were frozen at the level for the preceding year. Therefore, new programs could not be funded without eliminating existing programs and that was not a realistic alternative. Each program had a built-in constituency of workers and people served who resisted every effort to curtail, eliminate, or even evaluate their programs. Puerto Rican leaders understood the dilemma faced by black administrators but that did not make their task any easier. Understanding slowly turned to disappointment and finally to bitterness. It was at this point that some began to reason that Puerto Ricans would receive more benefits from a centralized program, administered by a white director or even City Hall; both of which, they felt, would be more responsive to their pressure.

Over the years Puerto Ricans in New York City have lost two-thirds of their citywide programs due to cutbacks. The black-Puerto Rican struggle continues in areas like Brownsville where forty percent

of the population is Puerto Rican but where blacks have firm control
of the Community Corporation board. In these cases, winner-takes-all
means not only a lack of jobs but also a lack of services for
Puerto Ricans. As programs become identified as being black or
Puerto Rican, the other group tends not to use them. Therein lies
one of the ironies, among many, in the tragic struggle between
blacks and Puerto Ricans over programs ostensibly designated to
alleviate the misery of poverty.

The Jewish Case

The Jewish case is replete with irony. For many years Jews gave
generously of their time and resources in support of the civil-
rights movement. Although the early days of the movement were not
free of tension between the races, much of the camaraderie and
good will was genuine as blacks and whites came together to
sing, plan, and act in buses, in meeting rooms, and on picket lines.
But events beyond the control of both groups were forcing changes
in the relationship.

The precise moment the civil-rights movement died is not known.
Some place the time shortly after the enactment of the 1964 Civil
Rights Act. It was clear by that time that the fight against de jure
segregation produced the "easy" victories, for the nation was
prepared to strike down such absurdities as separate drinking
fountains, separate waiting rooms in bus terminals, and segregated
lunch counters. But these victories did not materially change the
living conditions of most blacks. When it became apparent that the
de facto segregation and racism were intricately woven into the
fibers of our most cherished institutions, solutions became more
elusive. Blacks were prepared to abandon the interracial coalitions
that served a useful purpose during the formative years of the
movement and to assume full control of their struggle.

The late David Danzig, long associated with the American Jewish
Committee, explained the change in the following manner:

There are great differences between the civil-rights movement and
the "Negro Revolution," and these differences papered over so
long by certain historical exigencies are now surfacing into full
view. The civil-rights movement was and is essentially concerned
with the structure of law and social justice: its goals were
equality before the law and equality of individual opportunity.
As a movement it was begun by people whose aim was not to
aid the Negro as such but to bring American society into closer

conformity with constitutional principle. For the greatest part of its history, civil rights was the white liberal's cause. Liberals expounded the moral basis for human rights in religion and politics, developed the theory of human equality in the physical and social sciences, led the intellectual offensive against racism, and took the initiative in founding the civil-rights organizations. . . .

What changed civil rights almost overnight from a peripheral moral issue to our major domestic movement was the emergence of the Negroes themselves as a nationwide bloc.

As often is the case in sudden change, some were prepared for it and some were not. The targets of opportunity for black militants in the North were the white merchants, landlords, and teachers. In certain cities Jews were disproportionately represented in these target groups. As the incidents between the groups increased, some Jews felt betrayed while others felt all Jewry was under attack. If in the heat of battle an anti-Semitic remark was made, it soon overshadowed the original cause of the conflict. Thus black anti-Semitism became the issue rather than poor housing or inferior education.

It was, therefore, not surprising when the Anti-Defamation League of B'nai B'rith confirmed what many sensed: the Jewish community was turning inward away from non-Jewish affairs. A league survey among 2,500 American-Jewish leaders indicated an increasing concern over the lack of public indignation toward anti-Semitic manifestations causing many Jews to concentrate on their own interests and their own security. It is within this historical context that one can understand the release of a report critical of black control of the antipoverty program by the American Jewish Congress, a report that would not have been written five years before.

The Jewish case against the antipoverty program is well stated in the report that concentrated on the New York City experience but which the authors claim is applicable to other jurisdictions. The report estimates that there were about 250,000 indigent Jews in the city, comprising 15 percent of the poor, 60 percent of whom are over 60 years of age [1974]. Although the authors acknowledge the difficulty involved in identifying the Jewish poor, they state "unequivocally" that in spite of the large sums of money spent in fighting poverty, little of this money has gone to alleviate the plight of this group.

Reasons for the exclusion of Jews from the program are separated into two categories: those reasons external to the Jewish community

and the ones internal to it. Among the reasons external to the
Jewish community the report finds:

1. The OEO Act and federal guidelines emphasized a decentralized
system of specified poverty areas, as opposed to citywide programs. Many poor Jews do not live in these areas.
2. Agencies within the povery areas establish their programs to
serve not the entire area but one or more specific groups within
the population. Jews, numerically weak, tend to be ignored.
3. Agencies have failed to reach out to serve the poor outside
the pockets of poverty, although they are permitted to do so.
4. Low priority is given to programs serving the aged.
5. Poverty officials are unaware of Jewish poverty and are
more interested in servicing "their own."
6. The holding of elections for the governing boards of the
community corporations are held on the Jewish Sabbath.
7. Fear of physical abuse.
8. None of the criteria used to designate poverty areas is
descriptive of Jewish poverty.

Reasons for nonparticipation internal to the Jewish community
pertain to the lack of organization of the aged and lack of organization
on the local level. The feeling among Jewish organizations that the
poverty program belonged to blacks and Puerto Ricans is given as
another reason. Finally Jews have been "unable or reluctant to
engage in the 'politics of poverty'. . . .The traditional Jewish abhor-
rence of violence and of confrontation as a political weapon" has
discouraged Jews from pressing their demands.

Many of the biases described in the report are similar to
objections raised by the Puerto Ricans and Mexican Americans.
Therefore it is important to note the rationale that lead to some of
these biases. When attempting to tackle a problem as large and
as diverse in its manifestations as poverty, priorities must be
established. While political considerations are important ingredients
in this process, the decision to relegate programs serving the aged
to a low-priority status in favor of education and training programs
designed to serve children and young adults resulted not only in
a lack of services for several thousand indigent Jewish aged, but for
millions of black senior citizens as well. Similarly the practice of
stressing aid to black and Puerto Rican businessmen under Title IV
of the act can only be viewed as discrimination if one disagrees
with the premise that more mileage for the dollar can be realized
if minority businessmen are helped to establish and expand businesses
in impoverished areas where they reside. The American Jewish

Congress in fact helped to legitimatize this strategy when it joined with the Urban League to establish the Interracial Council for Business Opportunities to accomplish these same goals.

Although the report disclaims any "attempt to compete with other minority groups for the meager funds presently available to fight poverty," it calls for a more equitable distribution of funds and offers several schemes to accomplish this. Since the report contains no suggestion for a liberal coalition to seek adequate financing for all, the call for a more equitable distribution of curtailed funding can only be interpreted as an attempt to join the competition for program resources.

The fact that some Jews have suffered as a result of the evolutionary changes in black-white relationships is not doubted nor dismissed. But it must be stated that change is never orderly or equitable in either its rewards or penalties. This report, and the supporting evidence in the Anti-Defamation League survey, indicates that a segment of the Jewish leadership has turned inward. For years this leadership was ahead of its constituency, and, indeed, ahead of the nation in preaching tolerance and justice. This belief was, in part, self-serving, for it is based on the premise that only in a pluralistic society, built on tolerance and the acceptance of differences, can the Jewish community avoid assimilation and exist as a separate, viable entity. Perhaps constituent pressure demanded a change or perhaps the leaders no longer believe in the creed they have lived by so long. Nevertheless, it is difficult to see how Jewish security can be achieved at the expense of the largest minority group in the United States.

The Mexican-American Case

Historically, the relationship between blacks and Mexican Americans has been marked by competition and tension. Unlike the Jews and Puerto Ricans, Mexican Americans have not participated in sizable numbers in the civil-rights movement, although they have certainly been affected by it. Cultural factors and memories of vying for the scant amount of status, jobs, housing, and other resources successfully barred them from meaningful involvement in what they perceived to be a black cause. And yet as an urban people—a little recognized fact—Chicanos were likely candidates to compete with blacks in the cities of the Southwest for the urban-biased Great Society programs. Of the five million plus Mexican Americans concentrated in the states of Texas, New Mexico, Colorado, California, and Arizona, the overwhelming majority live in cities like Phoenix, East Los Angeles, Los Angeles, San Diego, San Francisco, Denver, Albuquerque, Austin, Corpus Christi, El Paso, and San Antonio.

The infusion of program resources into black communities in the Southwest was, for many Chicanos, another example of Anglo indifference to their plight. Surely, they argued, in terms of numbers and measurements of deprivation they could rival blacks, and in some areas exceed them, in qualifying for assistance. Some examples of what they perceived as discrimination in the distribution of funds illustrate their case:

The stepped up public and private aid channeled into Watts following the disorders there during the summer of 1965 stirred sharp resentment among Mexican-American leaders. Chicanos are the largest minority group in Los Angeles and generally regarded the Watts neighborhood superior to several of their own in this sprawling city.

A 1971 *Business Week* report in this same city quotes the director of the Minority Enterprise Small Business Investment Company as saying that Chicanos received only 35 percent of the poverty funds and control only 25 percent of the agencies distributing these funds.

In Santa Clara County, California, where Chicanos comprise 25 percent of the poor population and 50 percent of all the Aid to Dependent Children welfare cases, their leaders denounced the allocation of funds to the traditional service agencies in the area that they felt had a history of catering to the "less needy" blacks.

The more militant Chicano leaders soon realized that they could not compete with blacks for policymaking positions because they lacked the political clout that could make such appointments possible. President Johnson's response to Chicano demands resulted, in 1967, in the appointment of a six-member cabinet-level committee to study the ways the federal government could best work with state and local governments and private industry to improve conditions for Mexican Americans. The effort was followed by the largely unsuccessful White House Conference on Mexican Americans that same year.

The inability to influence national policy more meaningfully soon led to disenchantment with the handful of Mexican-American elected leaders whom the militants felt had not served them well. Thus the militants were soon fighting a three-front war—the Anglos, the blacks, and segments of the largely conservative Mexican-American communities. The elected officials, perhaps more attuned to the sentiments of their constituents, tried to discredit the militants by making disparaging comparisons between them and the blacks. Representative Henry B. Gonzales's 1968 attack is illustrative of this tactic:

> We see a strange thing in San Antonio today; we have those who play at revolution and those who imitate the militance of others—We have those who cry "brown power" only because they have heard "black power."

Undoubtedly the successes of the civil-rights and Black Power movements did not go unnoticed in the Chicano communities. At times the rhetoric was similar and analogies of the struggle of the two groups were made: Chicano leaders have labeled Denver and Del Rio their "Selma" and projected that East Los Angeles will be to the Chicanos in the seventies what Watts was to the blacks in the sixties. But great pains were taken by other segments of the Chicano leadership to emphasize the differences between themselves and blacks in their respective claims for justice. Some of these leaders rejected integration as a viable policy for Mexican Americans and began to stress their cultural heritage. A college student summed up this sentiment when he wrote:

> We're not like the Negroes. They want to be white men because they have no history to be proud of. My ancestors come from one of the most civilized nations in the world.

The fact that many Mexican Americans chose to assimilate or at least identify strongly with the dominant culture suggests that this view may be a minority opinion strategically used to win adherents to the more militant cause. However, other observers have also noticed the reaction of the populace when the term *La Raza* is evoked. Ralph M. Kramer noted in his comparative case studies on the antipoverty programs that part of the Chicano-black strain "was related to the difference in their social goals and their feelings of cultural superiority and distinctiveness." Their problems with blacks were seen as another chapter in their historic conflict with Anglos in the Southwest.

It appears that Chicanos will continue to look inward, kindle their own anger, and make their own demands. Blacks, at least for the present, will be seen as competitors rather than cohorts.

Conclusion: Strength from Within

The history of each of these minorities illustrates how initial hopes of alleviating the misery of poverty turned bitter as each became involved in an antiblack competitive drive to receive its share of Kennedy-Johnson program resources. Each not only suffered the loss of jobs and services but also the opportunity to force a powerful coalition capable of obtaining aid for their common problems.

The apparent success of President Nixon's drive to unilaterally eliminate or curtail many of these programs clearly suggests how self-defeating, for all groups, the competitive behavior has been. There are many factors that would explain this change in the national mood in less than a decade but the conflict surrounding the administration of these programs is an important consideration in any analysis of the situation.

The evidence we have uncovered indicates that blacks have little interest in forming coalitions if the price they must pay is to share limited program resources for an unspecified goal of intergroup harmony. Groups join coalitions to increase, not decrease, their influence. As the largest minority group in the country, blacks are consolidating power at the municipal level and increasingly see themselves exercising power on the national level. There is little talk among blacks of the use of disruption as a viable strategy to increase the flow of federal funds. Disruption has focused the nation's attention on black problems, but it has also brought repression. Funds received in direct response to fears of civil disorders, like those for summer recreation programs, hardly begin to address black priorities.

The events of the past decade have convinced the Puerto Ricans, Chicanos, and Jews that their best interests would be served if they turned inward. The former groups will attempt to build strong political and service organizations within their own communities, while the latter—having achieved these goals—will reassess past values and strategies. Most leaders spoke of a two-to-three-year period of ethnocentric preoccupation—sufficient time, it was hoped, to heal old wounds before an enduring coalition is possible.

The seeking of strength from within is a trend, not a monolithic movement and, of course, unforeseen events may bring the groups together sooner. Even today at the height of the tension, there is some cooperation taking place. Blacks and Puerto Ricans are working together in some school districts in New York City for greater representation on local school boards. A coalition of blacks, Chicanos, and liberal whites won all seven seats on the Houston (Texas) School Board in 1971. They almost succeeded in winning the mayorality election as well. There are probably many other examples of inter-group cooperation that will remain unheralded.

Recent attempts by Puerto Ricans and Chicanos to form a national alliance can be viewed as another indication of antiblack sentiment and in certain respects it is. But it is also a sign that the two groups recognize the fact that without blacks their chances to influence the political system on a national scale are diminished and this latest attempt is aimed at compensating for this weakness. Despite sharing a language and cultural background, there is little reason for these groups to unite since they do not share a common experience in this country. What they do share is a need for a common, national Spanish voice to bring their concerns to the nation's attention. With the Chicanos largely concentrated in the five Southwestern states and the Puerto Ricans situated mostly in the Northeast, an alliance has certain distinct advantages. The geo-graphic distance between them also provides fewer opportunities for the groups to compete for limited resources and thus lessens the chances for eruption of intergroup hostility. It should be noted, however, that all is not calm on the Puerto Rican-Chicano front. Officials in the Office of Spanish Surnames in Washington, D.C., for instance, report competition between the two minorities over the Elementary and Secondary Schools Act's Title VII funds. These monies, designated for bilingual programs for minority schoolchildren, are the source of friction between competing Chicano and Puerto Rican groups.

Instead of an extension of the antipoverty of the Model Cities programs, programs are needed to solve problems of structural poverty, like a guaranteed annual income, a full-employment program, a **vast**ly accelerated housing program, national health insurances, and increased federal aid to education. The dissolution of the liberal coalition during the second half of the Johnson administration and the Vietnam War foreclosed the possibility of enacting these programs, but they are natural extensions of the trends started in the 1960s. Even with direct American involvement in the war at an end, Congress was not likely to entertain such broad sweeping reforms in the absence of constituent pressure. The time to begin planning for a legislative assault is now. The first step is to establish a cooperative effort among groups.

An organization like the Leadership Conference on Civil Rights must begin the dialogue. Although the Conference membership does not represent all segments of the minority community, it offers some organizational stability. Recent attempts by groups like Common Cause, consumer advocate agencies, and environmental protection organizations have demonstrated that liberal reform can still attract wide support. Support from these groups will certainly be sought, but at this time they lack a significant number of minority-group members in their constituencies to serve as conveners of the desired forum.

There is some evidence that some black and white leaders have recognized the need for a broader coalition to advance minority goals. Senator Hubert H. Humphrey summarized the feelings of many in December 1972:

> I would argue that the civil-rights movement got into trouble when more and more people came to see it as an effort to give blacks a special break that was not afforded to other groups. The concept of civil rights must be broadened to include the rights and opportunities that should be available to other disadvantaged groups. Rather than a minority movement, this should be a movement based on economic enrichment of low-income and elderly people of all colors, and the minorities would benefit in the process. In the political arena there just aren't enough blacks, Chicanos, Indians, and Puerto Ricans to form an electoral majority. Over-emphasis on the needs of these identifiable groups can be and has been counterproductive.

These are not new sentiments—they have been stated and tried before. The task ahead for minorities is to call a cease-fire in the inner cities and to mobilize their forces to protect their interests. Unlike the past, they now have the political power to assure that they will not have minority status within the coalition. Within this context, new and former allies will be able to join them in promoting progressive legislation.

6

Attribution of Prejudice to Self and Others*

W. Curtis Banks, Janet L. Hubbard,
and Joseph S. Vannoy

Toward an understanding of interracial behavior and prejudice, research has been directed at assessing individual attitudes and their correlates (for example, see 11). The conceptual approach has been very simple; interracial behavior of individuals has been explained through an assessment of the attitudes that underlay it. Self-report techniques have offered a means for measuring individuals' perceptions of their own attitudes, though such reports often are inconsistent with behavior (8; 7) and are believed to be contaminated by motives that distort the perception and/or the presentation of self (for instance, social desirability motives; see 2). An alternative (though not opposing) approach to the issue of racial attitudes and behavior might involve an assessment of not only self-perceived prejudice, but also the extent to where individuals perceive others as prejudiced. Reference-group theory and the theory of social comparison (5) would suggest that the perception of racial attitudes and behavior on the part of others (especially close or "significant" others) may profoundly affect the attitudes and behavior of the individual. Although surprisingly little research has approached the

*The research reported here was supported in part by a National Institute of Mental Health grant, and a grant from the Social Science Research Council to W. C. Banks.

issue of prejudice from such a perspective, there is some evidence
that perceived social pressures may affect interracial behavior as
profoundly as personal attitudes (9).

One reason for inconsistencies in self-reported prejudice and
actual behavior may be the fact that such self-reports are viewed
by the individual as dispositional self-attributions. Indeed, prejudice
questionnaires are often labeled "Attitude Scale" and stress within
the instructions that attitudes and opinions are being measured.
Attribution theory (6) and/or some notion of social-desirability motives
would then lead one to expect relatively low self-attributed prejudice.
Individuals are not likely to see themselves as dispositionally responsible for even that level of prejudiced behavior that they are
aware of engaging in. On the other hand, others may be perceived
as generally more dispositionally motivated in their behavior. Thus,
the same level of prejudiced behavior in others (as it is in self) would
more readily be attributed to dispositional (attitudinal) factors in
others.

Moreover, even if we assume that individuals differ very little
from close associates and peers in behavior, we would predict that
attitude attributions will be greater for others than for self. Furthermore, if we follow Jones and Nisbett's notion about the informational
bases of self—other differences in attribution—we may predict that
close others (about whom an individual has more knowledge) will be
seen as less prejudiced than relatively distant (unfamiliar) others.

The implications of such a phenomenon are clear. Discrepancies
between self-reports and prejudiced behavior would be natural, in
that persons perceive the causes of their prejudiced behavior as
primarily situational rather than dispositional. Furthermore, the
perception of others as "genuinely" (dispositionally) prejudiced would
offer the normative support for prejudiced behavior that each individual claims constitutes his own situationality. A cyclic, social
process would then explain the persistence of prejudiced behavior,
the simultaneous denial of prejudiced attitudes, and the perception
that others are more prejudiced than self and constitute the social
structure that demands (or at least supports) one's own prejudiced
behavior.

The phenomenon of the "self-castigating racial liberal," who
confesses his own prejudiced attitudes, may also be explained. The
increased self-awareness and self-examination generated by the
pressures of changing norms (in the direction of nonprejudice) and
by the accusations of enraged blacks lead white individuals to perceive
their prejudiced behavior somewhat more objectively; or at least

to be more conscious and aware of it. This could lead to a tendency to perceive one's own prejudice as no less dispositional than the prejudice of others.

The first two studies reported here were directed at verifying the phenomenon (of self—other differences in attributed prejudice) suggested above, as well as its generality. The third investigation was directed at discerning whether the phenomenon of self—other differences in prejudice—reports is primarily a function of social desirability motives or some more basic process of attribution.

Study 1: Method

Questionnaire

The attitude questionnaire (4) consisted of 32 items to which subjects responded with the typical categories of strongly agree through strongly disagree, five in all. A response that is maximally prejudiced toward blacks would receive a score of 5 while a minimally prejudiced response would receive a score of 1. Thus, the maximum possible score, presumably reflecting a high degree of prejudice, is 160; the minimum score 32. On 13 of the items a positive response reflects a favorable orientation toward blacks and on 19 of the items a positive response reflects an unfavorable orientation, thus discouraging response stereotypy. Fendrich reports a split-half reliability for the scale of .91 (4).

Subjects

Five hundred eighteen undergraduates at Miami University in Ohio responded to this attitude scale in large classroom groups. Their participation was voluntary, and in return for "experimental" credits. The subject sample was made up predominantly of freshman students, from various departmental majors. Although some minority students participated in the study, their data was discarded.

Design and Procedure

Three experimental conditions were created by varying the instructions preceding the attitude questionnaire: attribution of attitudes to self, to close friends, or to the college-student population.

At the top of the questionnaire was the heading "Attitude Scale," to stress that Ss were indicating racial attitudes. In a section called

"Instructions," subjects read a brief statement to the effect that there were no right or wrong answers since the questions dealt with attitudes and opinions. Then one of the following statements was read:

1. "Self" Condition: "For every item, please mark *your* answer on the IBM sheet."
2. "Friends" Condition: "For every item, please mark on the IBM sheet the answer you feel *your closest friends would give.*"
3. "College Students" Condition: "For every item, please mark on the IBM sheet the answer you *feel most students here at Miami University would give.*"

Thus, by virtue of the instructions for answering the questionnaire, Ss were assigned to one of the experimental conditions. Assignment was random, the questionnaires having been intermixed prior to distribution to the classes.

Subjects were seated in a large classroom. The questionnaire and preceding instruction, covered with a blank sheet, were distributed to them. Ss were instructed to read the directions preceding the attitude questionnaire carefully. They indicated their responses to the scale items by placing a mark on an IBM answer sheet, at the top of which they indicated only their college class, sex, and race. The experimenter as well as his assistants were white, and it was made clear to the subjects that their responses were anonymous (they, in fact, deposited their completed questionnaires in a location remote from Es).

Study 1: Results

It was hypothesized that Ss who answered the racial-attitude scale for themselves would express less prejudice than the students who were attributing responses to either their closest friends or to "most college students." It was further hypothesized that racial prejudice would be attributed less to closest friends than to college students. The data support these hypotheses.

The overall mean score for subjects who answered the scale for themselves was 62.3. The overall mean score attributed to "closest friends" was 71.7. And the overall mean score attributed to "most college students" was 77.9 (see Table 1).

A one-way analysis of variance was performed on the data from the Fendrich scale. The results are presented in Table 2.

Table 1

Mean Self-, Friends-, and Student- Attributed Scores on Fendrich Scale

	Self	Closest Friends	Most Students	(Combined "Others")
Study 1	62.26	71.69	77.93	(75.04)
Study 2	58.81	64.96	74.55	(69.76)
Study 3	55.06	59.21	62.65	(60.73)

Table 2

Analysis of Variance of Fendrich Scale Scores—Study 1

Source	SS	df	MS	F
TOTAL	243082	517		
BETWEEN:				
Instructions	22232.50	2	11116.25	25.92, p .001
Contrast	21106.43	1	21106.43	49.22, p .001
Residual	1126.07	1	1126.07	2.63 n.s.
ERROR	220849.50	515	428.830	0

The effect of the instruction manipulation was significant (F = 25.92, p < .001). A specific-contrast analysis reflecting the hypothesis that Ss would attribute less prejudice to self than to close friends, and less to close friends than to college students, yields an F of 49.22 (p < .001) with a nonsignificant residual variance (F = 2.63). (The contrast used throughout the analysis reported here reflected the hypothesis that subjects would attribute least prejudice to themselves than to friends and most to college students.)

Study 2: Method

The second study was undertaken to determine: the generalizability of the results of the first experiment beyond the subject population at Miami University; and whether a repeated-measures design would render the same differential attribution to self and others as the between-subject design.

The Fendrich scale (described above) was again used as the primary dependent measure (4). In addition, subjects responded to a number of direct questions aimed at discovering the extent to which they perceived prejudice in themselves, their friends, and "most students" to be representative of underlying feelings and opinions. We predicted that individuals would tend to perceive their own overall prejudice as less dispositional than that of others. Also, responses to these questions offered us direct ratings of self and others in overall as well as dispositional prejudice.

Subjects

Sixty students from an "Introduction to Psychology" course at California State University, Hayward, were subjects in the experiment. Participation was voluntary and in return for "experimental" credit. Although nonwhite subjects engaged in the experiment, their data were not used.

Design and Procedure

The experimental design consisted of three repeated measures on the Fendrich Attitude Scale. Each S answered the scale once for "self," once for "closest friends," and once for "most Cal. State students." Order of instruction modes was completely counter-balanced. All subjects answered a short additional questionnaire placed at the end of their booklets. On this questionnaire Ss rated their own, their closest friend's, and most students' overall prejudice, and prejudiced feelings and opinions on a scale from one (not at all prejudiced) to five (very prejudiced).

All the instructions for answering the Fendrich scales and the short questionnaire were written in the booklets that the subjects received. Ss were instructed to answer the Fendrich scale each time independently, without regard to previous responses. The experimenter and his assistants were white. And the anonymity of Ss's responses was stressed, as they were in Study 1.

Study 2: Results

Fendrich Scale

Mean scores on the Fendrich scale for the three experimental conditions can be seen in Table 1. A one-way repeated-measures analysis of variance was performed on the Fendrich scores with the results appearing in Table 3. The effect of instruction mode was highly significant, yielding an F of 14.19 (p < .001).

Table 3

Analysis of Variance of Fendrich
Scale Scores—Study 2

Source	SS	df	MS	F
TOTAL	66969.78	179		
Between Ss	28052.45	59		
Within Ss	38917.33	120		
Instructions	7544.00	2	3772.00	14.19, p < .001
Contrast	7432.43	1	7432.43	27.95, p < .001
Residual	111.57	1	111.57	< 1
ERROR	31373.33	118	265.88	

A specific-contrast analysis reflecting the hypothesis of self > friends > college-students attribution of prejudice was performed, yielding an F of 27.95 (p < .001) and a nonsignificant residual (F < 1).

Responses to the additional questionnaire were scored and analyzed separately from the Fendrich data. The means appear in Table 4. Subjects rated themselves as less prejudiced overall than friends, and friends less than students (F contrast = 20.18, p < .001). More specifically, subjects rated themselves as dispositionally (feelings and opinions) less prejudiced than friends, and friends as less dispositionally prejudiced than students (F contrast = 22.37, p < .001).

In addition, differences in overall and dispositional prejudice ratings were computed for self, friends, and students. The data suggest that Ss perceived their feelings and opinions as different from (more favorable than) their overall prejudice (behavior, and so forth) (t = 2.02, p < .05), while they rated the overall prejudice and prejudiced feelings of friends (t = 1.85) and students (t = 1.64) as nondifferential. However, an analysis of variance of these difference scores did not yield a significant value for a pattern of self > friends > students differentiation in overall versus dispositional prejudice ratings.

Table 4

Mean Ratings of Self, Friends, and College Students on Overall Prejudice, Prejudiced Feelings, and Social Pressures toward Prejudice

		Overall Prejudice	Prejudiced Feelings	Social Pressures
	Self	2.25	2.05	——
Study 2*	Friends	2.75	2.57	——
	Students	2.83	2.73	——
	Self	5.30	5.30	4.53
Study 3**	Friends	5.29	5.17	3.73
	Students	4.84	4.72	3.43

*Low scores indicate low prejudice ratings.
**High scores indicate low prejudice ratings.

Study 3: Method

The first two investigations offer consistent support for a pattern of differential attribution of prejudice to self and others. However, an explanation of that pattern is not altogether clear. Although the experimental procedure was designed to minimize self-consciousness and ego-defensiveness (through anonymity and the use of white experimenters), social-desirability motives may yet account for the tendency to attribute less racial prejudice to self than to friends or to "most students." An alternative explanation would be in terms of attribution theory—subjects see themselves as less (than others) dispositionally motivated and thus less prejudiced.

A black experimenter would likely increase self-awareness and ego-defensiveness. Subjects are likely to be much more self-conscious in their racial behavior (especially self-reports) in the presence of a black than in the presence of a white (12). If social-desirability motives alone underlay the attribution patterns found in the first two studies, we may expect that the presence of a black experimenter would lead subjects to present an even more favorable, unprejudiced image of themselves relative to others. We should expect, then, that a black experimenter would maximize a need to attribute less prejudice to self than to others.

Alternately, an attributional scheme would suggest that heightened self-consciousness might make individuals' perception of themselves more like perception of others (3). Within one informational model of attribution, Jones and Nisbett suggest that attentiveness to others as salient objects increases the tendency of persons to make more dispositional attributions to others than to self. Self-consciousness may increase self-attentiveness, and thus lead to a decrease in the differential attribution of prejudice to self and others. These alternative hypotheses were tested in the third study.

Undergraduates enrolled in an introductory psychology course at Princeton University were asked to complete a questionnaire. A black experimenter requested that Ss cooperate in answering the attitude scale included in the packets that were passed around. All of the subjects participated simultaneously in a large classroom. The attitude scale was the Fendrich, used in Studies 1 and 2. The instructions to answer the scale for "self," for "closest friends," or for "most students" were varied among subjects. Thus each subject answered the Fendrich scale once, according to the instruction mode written on his form. In addition, each subject answered the following three questions within the same instruction mode as he/she responded to the Fendrich scale:

1. How would you rate _____ in overall prejudice (behavior, and so on) toward blacks?
2. How would you rate the feelings and opinions of_____toward blacks?
3. To what extent do you feel social pressures and expectations (parents, peers, and so on) account for _____ overall prejudiced behavior?

Responses to these items were indicated on a scale from 1 (entirely or extremely prejudiced) to 7 (not at all [prejudiced]).

Study 3: Results

The mean scores on the Fendrich scale for the three experimental conditions appear in Table 1. Although an analysis of variance shows no significant overall main-effect differences in prejudice attributed to "self," "friends," and "most students" (F = 2.14, n.s.), a specific contrast indicates that the pattern of prejudice attributions hypothesized and supported in the first two studies has been replicated here (F = 4.04, p < .05).

Mean differences in prejudice scores attributed to self and to others (combined friends and students) were computed for the data in this study and in the previous replications. A comparison of these differences reveals that Ss in the present study (black E) differentiated less in attributions to self versus others than subjects in Study 1 (t = 3.82, p < .001) or Study 2 (t = 2.20, p < .03).

Mean scores on the three-item questionnaire that followed the Fendrich scale appear in Table 4. Subjects did not rate themselves overall as less prejudiced than friends or most students (F = 2.62). While subjects rated their own feelings and opinions (dispositions) as somewhat less prejudiced than friends' or students' (F = 3.97, p < .05), they also rated the effects of social pressures (environmental factors) as greater upon friends and students than upon self (F = 11.54, p. <.001). These findings suggest that Ss in the present study may have rated themselves as more dispositionally similar to others than subjects in Study 2. Although this trend was found in the data, it failed to reach significance at an acceptable level. It may be worthwhile to note, however, that a situation- (social pressure) disposition- (feelings) causal index of perceived prejudice (computed from the second and third questions) showed no differences in the extent to which prejudice was seen as dispositionally versus situationally caused in self and others (F = 2.83).

Discussion

Throughout the three studies reported here a consistent pattern was found for attributions of prejudiced attitudes to self and to others. In each case, self was rated as less prejudiced than friends or students, while friends were rated as less prejudiced than students. One might offer interpretations of such a phenomenon based either upon social-desirability motives or a theory of attribution, though these explanations are not entirely independent. The evidence in Study 3 offers strong support for an attributional explanation.

When subjects completed the attitude scale in the presence of a black experimenter, the differentiation of self and others was replicated, but in a significantly reduced magnitude. This implies that the effect of a black experimenter was to decrease the differences in perception of self versus others, rather than to enhance ego motives to differentiate between self and others to a greater degree. We may tentatively infer from this finding that the primary process underlying the pattern of attitude reports here was one of person-perception and attribution.

Individuals generally perceive the causes of their own prejudiced behavior as less attitudinal and dispositional than the behavior of friends or students. Furthermore, more familiar others (friends) are seen as less dispositional than relatively unfamiliar others (students). Such an interpretation of the findings is consistent with current theory regarding actor and observer attributions (6). We may assume that a black E had the effect of making subjects perceive themselves more similarly to the manner in which they perceive others (through self-consciousness and self-attentiveness). However, we may not rule out the effects of social-desirability motives altogether. It is interesting to note that subjects achieved self-other similarity in perceived prejudice by perceiving others as less prejudiced (less dispositional or more situational) rather than by perceiving self as more prejudiced (dispositional), than in the previous replications.

The data from the direct questions that subjects answered in Studies 2 and 3 offer supportive evidence for the phenomenon and for our interpretation. In Study 2, subjects rated themselves as less prejudiced overall than friends, and friends less than students. In Study 3, subjects rated themselves and others as not different in overall prejudice. In both studies, subjects rated themselves as less dispositionally prejudiced than friends or students, though to a much lesser degree in Study 3. In addition, subjects in Study 2 rated their dispositional prejudice as significantly less than their overall self-rated prejudice, while they rated the feelings and opinions of others as consistent with their (others') overall prejudice. Furthermore, a dispositional-situational causal index derived from subjects' ratings in Study 3 showed no difference in the attributions made regarding the prejudice of self and others. Indeed, on the situational measure alone, subjects rated their own prejudice as less situational than the prejudice of others (indicating a pattern of attribution for others that is typical of normal self-attributions). This last point may account for the fact that friends and students were seen as relatively unprejudiced in Study 3 (on the Fendrich scale).

Unfortunately, one valuable measure is absent from these investigations. A measure of dispositional and situational ratings by subjects in all three replications would offer more conclusive evidence of the attributional shift in Study 3. Still, the pattern of findings is so consistent and significant that the interpretations made here, with the supportive evidence, seem most plausible. Further extension of this research may utilize laboratory paradigms in which more controlled manipulations of variables affecting attitude attributions may be made. Toward a more general theory of attitude attributions, replications of this research should also be extended into attitude dimensions other than racial prejudice.

For the present, our findings offer important implications for self-attribution and the nature of prejudice. One implication is that self-reported attitudes may not be simple descriptions of behavior. Rather, they are careful inferences of the dispositionality of one's own behavior, especially when that dispositionality has important social-approval consequences (as witnessed in the case of racial prejudice).

The compelling practical implications of these findings have to do with the specific phenomenon of prejudice and the general issue of social change. If individuals fail to perceive themselves as the source of unapprovable attitudes and behavior, it is not likely that they will attempt social change through self-examination. It is probable that many forms of prejudiced behavior are elicited and maintained by situational factors such as implicit social norms (10; 1; 9) and the perception that every other person not only conforms in action but also in sentiment. An effective attempt at social progress through behavior and attitude change, therefore, would need to be directed at convincing each individual that the social-situational supports of behavior are changing, that others are shifting in their dispositions, and that he/she must consider those prerogatives (perhaps based upon dispositional factors) which he/she has to freely act outside the influence of perceived norms.

References

1. Campbell, D. T. 1963. "Social Attitudes and Other Acquired Behavioral Dispositions." In *Psychology: A Study of a Science*. Edited by S. Koch. New York: McGraw-Hill.
2. Crowne, D. P., and Marlow, D. 1964. *The Approval Motive*. New York: Wiley.
3. Duval, S., and Wicklund, R. A. 1973. "Effects of Objective Self-awareness on Attribution of Causality." *Journal of Experimental Social Psychology* 9:17-31.
4. Fendrich, J. M. 1967. "A Study of the Association among Verbal Attitudes, Commitment, and Overt Behavior in Different Experimental Situations."

Social Forces 45:347-55.

5. Festinger, L. 1954. "A Theory of Social Comparison Processes." *Human Relations* 2:119-40.

6. Jones, E. E., and Nisbett, R. E. 1972. "The Actor and the Observer: Divergent Perceptions of the Causes of Behavior." In *Attribution: Perceiving the Causes of Behavior*. Edited by E. E. Jones, et al. Morristown, N. J.: General Learning Press.

7. Kutner, B.; Wilkins, C.; and Yarrow, P. 1952. "Verbal Attitudes and Overt Behavior Involving Racial Prejudice," *Journal of Abnormal and Social Psychology* 47:649-52.

8. La Piere, R. T. 1934. "Attitudes versus Actions." *Social Forces* 13:230-37.

9. Mezei, L. 1971. "Perceived Social Pressure as an Explanation of Shifts in Relative Influence of Race and Beliefs on Prejudice across Social Interactions." *Journal of Personality and Social Psychology* 19:69-81.

10. Minard, R. D. 1952. "Race Relationships in the Pocahontas Coal Field." *Journal of Social Issues* 8:29-44.

11. Rokeach, M. 1968. *Beliefs, Attitudes, and Values*. San Francisco: Jossey-Bass.

12. Summers, G., and Hammonds, A. 1966. "Effect of Racial Characteristics of the Investigator on Self-enumerated Responses to a Negro Prejudice Scale." *Social Forces* 44, no. 4:515.

7

Racial Attitudes of
Native-American Preschoolers

Ann H. Beuf

The present study focuses on Native-American and white preschool children and their feelings about race (many American
Indians prefer to have the term *Native Americans* applied to their
group). It is a replication of studies that have been carried out with
black and white youngsters. Most of the children in the sample are
reservation children. They have been surrounded by other Native
Americans; children who have attended preschool have been in all
Native-American classes. Thus, their exposure to outright prejudice
of a personal nature has been minimal. No one has made fun of
their race at school, no neighbor has refused to let a precious
offspring play with them because of their race. However, the children
have, through television and their own observations, begun to see
what roles in society are occupied by whom. This raises an interesting
question for the student of race relations. In the past, sociologists
indicated that if minority-group children were adversely affected
by their status, it was because of personal hurt inflicted by prejudiced
others. Yet investigators have not attempted to separate out that
kind of personal influence and the influence of the simple awareness
of the social structure. The hypothesis of this research is that
institutional patterns and not personal experience with prejudice is
the major factor influencing the racial attitudes of the minority-
group child—in this case the Native American. Because of the

isolated condition in which many of these children live, any evidence of low racial self-esteem on their part is not due to personal hurt, but to institutional racism.

Methods

The technique employed in the study was a replication of the Porter doll-play and storytelling test, developed for the study of the racial attitudes of Boston children in the 1960s (17). The test was modified to some extent to create situations with which the Native-American children could better identify. For example, while the second story that Porter used as a birthday story and most of the characters were children, I included more adult characters, because many birthday celebrations among Native Americans are intergenerational events.

The interviewer involves the child in telling a story. The plot is structured, but certain roles in the story are "open." This means that it is up to the child to select which of the two dolls will "be" the person in the story. For example, in the first story the child is asked to select "a good friend," "a nice girl that they like to play with," "the kid they don't like," and "the kid who can be invited home for lunch." The second story involves the choice of "Dad's good friend," "a clean and neat girl," and "the person to whom the hero (heroine) wishes to give some soda pop." Small flexible dolls are used in the test. Half of them are fair skinned and blond and the other half light brown skinned and dark haired with slightly upturned eyes. A "set" consists of two dolls dressed identically and differing only in racial characteristics. As the points in the story approach when the child must select a doll to fill one of the stereotyped roles in the story, the interviewer presents a set of dolls to the child, from which he/she selects one to "be" the person in the story. Two stories were told. The first is about a child's morning in school and employed a schoolroom set of doll furniture; the second story, about a birthday celebration, utilized a set of simple living-room furniture. Racial preference was measured by the number of times a child selected a doll of his/her own racial group to play a positive role in the story or a doll of the other race to play a negatively stereotyped role. A child was given a + 1 for a choice that indicated a positive stereotype of his/her own race, and if, on the one negative item (the kid they do not like to play with) they selected a doll of the other race. (There is no implication here that to like one's own group means a dislike of the other group or that dislike of one's own group means liking of the other group. Rather, these choices in a force-choice situation represent a rough measure of racial stereotypy.) For example, if a Native-American child selected the darker doll to play the role of the "kid people like to play with," he would receive a score of + 1. If, on the other hand, he selected the white doll, he received 0 on that item. Since there were eight questions that tapped the preference aspect of the children's attitudes, the highest possible score would be + 8. To facilitate comparison with the Porter data, the preference scores were collapsed into three categories—"high" or + 3 for children who scored + 7 or + 8, "medium" or + 2 for subjects who scored between + 4 and + 6, and "low" or + 1 for scoring less than a + 4.

In the case of racial self-identification, the child was told at the beginning of each of the two stories, "This story is about a little boy (girl) who looks like you. Which one of these two dolls looks the most like you?" Those children who correctly identified themselves twice were given a score of two (2). Subjects who misidentified once or both times received a score of one (1). Thus, for a child to be considered a correct identifier, he or she had to show a consistent perception of racial membership and willingness to acknowledge that fact. One incorrect choice could not be considered correct since it is indicative of ambivalance on the part of the child.

In addition, a cognitive test of the child's color-matching ability was incorporated into the game. He was asked to match cards on which were colorful pictures of Native Americans, blacks, and whites, to the Native-American and white dolls. This had the same purpose as the doll-family matching test used by Porter, but avoided the contaminating use of the word *family*; because the color range in many Native-American families is quite large, I could not safely assume that failure to make a family of all brown dolls would really indicate the child's lack of awareness of color differences. It might simply be an accurate reflection of his/her own family composition. This test, while more stringent than the family matching, still correlated highly with the doll-matching test and thus appears to be a valid assessment of the children's ability to match by color.

At the end of the game, the children were asked to place the dolls back in their boxes. As they picked up the dolls, the interviewer pointed to the four dolls representing adult females (two white and two brown). "Which of these women are Indians?" she asked the child. This gave some indication of the term knowledge of the children and served to generate spontaneous remarks, especially on the part of the white youngsters.

The doll-play technique is especially suited for work with young children because it involves them in play with the dolls and gives them freedom to move about. The equipment is colorful and holds their interest throughout the half-hour interview, thus helping to prevent superficial or disinterested responses.

The relationship between the dependent variables of racial preference and racial self-identification and the independent variables of race awareness, age, and race were examined in a sample of 117 Native-American children and a control group of 95 white youngsters. (Racial preference was also considered as an independent variable with regard to its effect on racial self-identification.) The control group was selected to resemble the Native-American group in preschool age and geographical location. An attempt was made to obtain as many white children of working and lower socioeconomic class as possible. However, the control group does contain a larger percent of middle-class children than the Native-American group. (A control for social class indicated that the results by race hold when that variable is held constant.) This is largely due to the problems of locating middle-class Native Americans, of whom there are very few. Of the Native-America children, 55 were members of a Southwestern agricultural group in Arizona, 20 from a Dakota plains tribe, and 42 were members of a Nebraska plains tribe, half of whom were living on their home reservation and the other half were living in an urban area. Within the Native-American group, the effects of tribe, appearance, parental activism, and urban versus reservation residence were also examined.

Inevitably in such research the question of the race of the interviewer is raised (12). In this study, twenty of the Southwestern Native-American children were tested by a Native-American interviewer. Her results did not differ significantly (and show small numerical difference) from the results of the white, female author with a group of children matched for race, age, sex, and socioeconomic status. In fact, there was a slight tendency for children to identify themselves better with the white tester, although all differences between the two sets of children were too minimal to be considered significant (2). In all cases, the interviewer visited homes and schools at least once before coming to interview the children, so that she was someone with whom the children were familiar.

Results

Between Races

The most important results were found in the relationship between race and the children's racial preference and racial self-identification.

Native-American children showed less preference for the dolls of their own race than did white children and less tendency to identify themselves correctly. Both are highly statistically significant (see Tables 1 and 2).

Table 1

Mean-preference Scores of Native-American (Indian) and White Children of Younger and Older Preschool Age Groups

Race	Age	
	3-4	5-low 6
White	1.84 (N = 76)	2.15 (N = 19)
Indian	1.66 (N = 69)	1.54 (N = 48)

F Age = 1.13 (n.s.)   N = 212
F Race = 19.56 p < .001
F Age x Race = 6.06 p < .01

Table 2

Mean Racial Self-identification Scores of Native-American (Indian) and White Children of Younger and Older Preschool Age Groups

Race	Age	
	3-4	5-low 6
White	1.53 (N = 76)	1.84 (N = 19)
Indian	1.43 (N = 69)	1.37 (N = 48)

                                                               N = 212

F Age = 2.44 (n.s.)
F Race = 13.55 p < .001
F Age x Race = 5.44 p < .05

In addition, while age increases the preference for own race in whites and also the tendency to identify with the doll of one's own race, this pattern is not obtained for Native-American youngsters. In fact, the reverse is true. The strength of the age-race interaction F reveals that preference for *white* and identification with it increase in the older Native-American group. These patterns suggest that the more a child learns of the world and his place in it, the more conscious he or she becomes of white as the preferred status.

In addition, the Native-American group's performance cannot be attributed to lack of cognition of racial awareness. The findings here are similar to Porter's results with her black and white sample. Self-identification is strongly related to stereotypy/preference but is *not* related strongly to the measure of cognition—the picture to doll-color matching described above (see Tables 3 and 4). Thus it appears that attitudes—as measured by the doll choice for stereotyped roles—exerts the stronger influence on a child's racial self-identification than does his intellectual awareness of color differences and the ability to match by color.

Table 3

Mean Racial Self-identification Scores for Total Sample, by Doll-to-picture Making Scores *

Doll-to-picture Matching Scores	N	Mean Self-identification Score
0	30	1.40
1	89	1.44
2	93	1.58

N = 212

F = 2.19 (n.s.)

*Key to scoring on doll-to-picture matching: 0—child was unable to correctly match the white doll to white picture or Indian doll to Indian picture; 1—child correctly matched one of the dolls to the correct picture, but mismatched the other; 2—child was able to correctly match both dolls to the correct pictures.

Table 4

Mean Racial Self-identification Scores for Total Sample by Racial Preference Scores

Preference Scores	N	Mean Self-identification Score
1 (low)	70	1.30
2 (medium)	126	1.54
3 (high)	16	1.87

N = 212

F = 11.65 p. < .01

Within the Native-American Group

Holding tribe constant and examining the performance of the Nebraska plains tribe's urban and reservation children, it was found that the reservation children tended to show higher own-race preference and self-identification. Reservation children are exposed to the presence of a large all Native-American peer group, which probably serves to draw them more closely into the Native-American community in a Durkeimian sense and to identify themselves with it (see Tables 5 and 6).

Table 5

Own-race Preference by Resident
1 = low
3 = high

Residence	N	Mean Preference Score
Urban	21	1.57
Reservation	21	1.68

N = 42
F = .45 (n.s.)

Table 6

Self-identification by Residence
1 = low
2 = high

Residence	N	Mean Self-identification Score
Urban	21	1.33
Reservation	21	1.50

N = 42
F = 1.71 (n.s.)

The urban child, on the other hand, is often the only Native-American child in his neighborhood and may be teased or in other ways victimized by whites. Several mothers informed me of disquieting incidents that had occurred in the neighborhood or at school.

In addition, urban children are more frequently exposed to the unfavorable image of the Native-American group projected by the media.

Interpretation of the Results

I began by stating that the hypothesis of this study was that institutional patterns, rather than painful personal experience with prejudice, is the major factor in influencing the racial preference of the minority-group child—in this case the Native American. If first-hand experience with racial prejudice were the cause of low own-race prejudice, then one should not expect to find that phenomenon among Native-American children, most of whom have had little contact with whites. Nonetheless, such a phenomenon is found among the children in the sample. Therefore it appears that a perception of the *role structure* of our society is sufficient to influence the racial attitudes of these children. Further support for this argument comes from the consideration of the age x race interaction data. The older a white child gets, the more he realizes that he is part of the powerful segment of society, while the older the Native-American child becomes, the more he realizes that his people are poor, unable to get jobs, and powerless compared to whites. A similar relationship manifests itself among matching ability, race, and the dependent variables of own-race preference and racial self-identification. In other words, the more a Native-American child knows about race, the more likely he is to see his own race in a poor light, while the reverse is true for whites.

The results of the urban-reservation difference in the Nebraska tribe indicate that the urban children who must face prejudice and rejection as well as learn the hierarchical map of society are even more adversely affected than the reservation youngsters.

Implications

In the past several years solutions have been directed by the theory that the suffering of outright personal discrimination causes damage to the self-esteem of minority-group children. Thus, it is assumed if white attitudes get better (as indeed Pettigrew has indicated they have), fewer minority children will suffer such incidents and all will be well.

In addition, the "black is beautiful" movement has aimed at increasing the pride of black youngsters in their own appearance and in their cultural heritage. Two other trends, the ghettoization of the cities and the ideology of black separatism, have created islands of blackness in white society—islands that are protective in part. The children on these islands are surrounded by other blacks, attend school with other blacks, and play with other blacks. They are protected to a large extent from hurting incidents to which I have referred. But does this description of the lives of black youngsters sound like a rerun of the description of the lives of Native-American reservation children? It is meant to, because the two situations are coming to resemble each other more and more.

But it must be remembered that those reservation children showed low own-race preference and low racial self-identification. This indicates that cultural insulation is not enough. And what is more, you cannot easily deceive or "con" children. They are perceptive little creatures who are busily assemblying the picture puzzle of the social world. An all Native-American play group does not prevent the child's realization that all the important people on television are white, or that the Bureau of Indian Affairs officials who exert great control over his parents and their friends are white. Similarly, the cry of "black is beautiful" alone cannot blind the black child to white power and black powerlessness in the economic and political worlds.

We must begin to turn our efforts to combating institutional racism—to altering the role structure of society that our children are absorbing. The way to develop positive attitudes toward his or her own race in the minority-group child would appear to be in providing that child with a view of society in which the hierarchy of power was not correlated with that of race. When the minority-group child perceives a world where his or her people are well represented in all roles, especially the ones that bring with them respect and self-determination as well as a diminishment of prejudice, we shall find minority-group children who truly value their racial membership and actively identify with it.

References

1. Anderson, James G., and Safar, Dwight. 1967. "The Influence of Differential Community Perceptions on the Provision of Equal Educational Opportunities." Sociology of Education 40 (Summer):219-30. Also in Native Americans Today: Sociological Perspectives. Edited by Howard M. Bahr, Bruce A. Chadwick, and Robert C. Day. 1972. New York: Harper and Row, pp. 69-79.
2. Beuf, Ann H. 1972. "Inner Alcatraz: Racial Preference and Racial Self-identification in Preschool White and American Indian Children." Ph.D. dissertation, Bryn Mawr College.
3. Bowker, Lee H. 1972. "Red and Black in Contemporary American History Texts: A Content Analysis." In Native Americans Today: Sociological Perspectives. Edited by Howard M. Bahr, Bruce A. Chadwick, and Robert C. Day. New York: Harper and Row, pp. 101-109.
4. Clark, Kenneth, and Clark, Mamie. 1939. "The Development of Consciousness of Self and the Emergence of Racial Identity in Negro Preschool Children." Journal of Social Psychology 10:591-99.
5. Clark, Kenneth, and Clark, Mamie. 1958. "Racial Identification and Preference in Negro Children." In Readings in Social Psychology. Edited by Eleanor E. Maccoby, Theodore M. Newcomb, and Eugene Hartley. New York: Holt, Rinehart, and Winston, pp. 602-611.
6. Fuchs, Estelle, and Havighurst, Robert J. 1972. To Live on This Earth. Garden City, N.Y.: Doubleday.
7. Goodman, Mary Ellen. 1952. Race Awareness in Young Children. Reading, Mass.: Addison-Wesley.
8. Gregor, James A., and McPherson, D. A. 1966. "Racial Preference and Ego Identity among White and Bantu Children in the Republic of South Africa." Genetic Psychology Monographs 73:218-53.
9. Houts, Kathleen, and Bahr, Rosemary S. 1972. "Stereotyping of Indians and Blacks in Magazine Cartoons." In Native Americans Today: Sociological Perspectives. Edited by Howard M. Bahr, Bruce A. Chadwick, and Robert C. Day. New York: Harper and Row, pp. 110-114.

10. Hraba, J., and Grant, Geoffrey. 1970. "Black Is Beautiful: A Reexamination of Racial Attitudes." *Journal of Personality and Social Psychology* 16, no. 3 (November):398-401.
11. Johnson, Helen W. 1969. "Rural Indian Americans in Poverty." Economic Research Service, U.S. Department of Agriculture. Agricultural Economic Report no. 167. Washington, D.C.: U.S. Government Printing Office. Also in *Native Americans Today: Sociological Perspectives*. Edited by Howard M. Bahr, Bruce A. Chadwick, and Robert C. Day. 1972. New York: Harper and Row, pp. 24-30.
12. Katz, Irwin; Robinson, James; Epps, Edgar; and Waly, Patricia. 1964. "The Influence of Race of the Experimenter and Instructions upon the Expression of Hostility by Negro Boys." *Journal of Social Issues* 20 (April):54-59.
13. Levitan, Sar, and Hetrick, Barbara. 1971. *Big Brother's Indian Programs: With Reservations*. New York: McGraw-Hill.
14. Luebben, Ralph A. 1964. "Prejudice and Discrimination against Navajos in a Mining Community." *The Kiva* 30 (October):1-17. Also in *Native Americans Today: Sociological Perspectives*. Edited by Howard M. Bahr, Bruce A. Chadwick, and Robert C. Day. 1972. New York: Harper and Row, pp. 89-101.
15. Morland, Kenneth. 1963. "Racial Self-identification: A Study of Nursery-school Children." *American Catholic Sociological Review* 24:591-99.
16. Pettigrew, Thomas. 1971. *Racially Separate or Together?* New York: McGraw-Hill, pp. 165-203.
17. Porter, Judith D. R. 1971. *Black Child, White Child*. Cambridge, Mass.: Harvard University Press.
18. Wahrhaftig, Albert L., and Thomas, Robert K. 1969. "Renaissance and Repression: The Oklahoma Cherokee." *Society* 6, no. 4 (February): 42-48. Also in *Native Americans Today: Sociological Perspectives*. Edited by Howard M. Bahr, Bruce A. Chadwick, and Robert C. Day. 1972. New York: Harper and Row, pp. 80-89.
19. Wax, Rosalie H. 1972. "The Warrior Dropouts." In *Native Americans Today: Sociological Perspectives*. Edited by Howard M. Bahr, Bruce A. Chadwick, and Robert C. Day, New York: Harper and Row, pp. 146-54.

8

Institutional Racism: A Perspective in Search of Clarity and Research

Nijole Benokraitis and Joe Feagin

Introduction

Despite the decline of both legal and physical segregation, blacks are still in a grossly unequal position within most institutions.* Racial stratification persists. Currently, racial inequality cannot be attributed solely to ideological racism, ethnocentrism, or behavior motivated solely by antiblack prejudice. Subordination techniques such as slavery and legal segregation are also no longer applicable. Instead, exclusionary practices have emerged that function to limit black access to such social benefits as power, prestige, and wealth. Such inequality may be grouped into two broad categories—inequality that is due to behavior based on antiblack prejudice and inequality due to behavior that is not based on antiblack prejudice.

For the most part, the theoretical perspectives that emerged during the first half of the twentieth century analyzed the former type of inequality in racial and ethnic relations. Until the mid-1950s white-nonwhite relationships were examined largely in terms of attitudes and stereotypes. The emphasis on prejudice has been pervasive

*We would like to thank S. Dale McLemore, Parker Frisbie, Ed Murguia, and Edna Bonacich for their critical comments on an earlier version of this manuscript. Partial support for this research came from a Ford Foundation Dissertation Fellowships in Ethnic Studies grant.

despite the introduction in "assimilation models" and "caste-class models" of such structural factors as economic competition, spatial segregation, the protection of vested interests, and the legal enforcement of differential privileges and obligations. Stimulated largely by the *Brown vs. Board of Education* decision in 1954 and its ramifications for changing attitudes as well as behavior, discrimination became an analytical and empirical source of sociological interest in the late 1950s and remained so through the 1960s. Discussions of discrimination were interspersed with typological approaches focusing on single or multiple variables and with such competing perspectives as "conflict models" and "pluralism models."

It is not our purpose here to discuss the broad array of theoretical and typological perspectives that have been utilized to describe dominant-minority relations. It will suffice to point out that, until the mid-1960s, emphasis was placed on attitudinal variables, that the behavioral discussion was often limited to consideration of "individual racism" or "individual discrimination." The focus shifted in the late 1960s, however, and a new theoretical perspective— "institutional racism"—emerged attempting to explain intergroup relations. The writers associated with developing this perspective have included Carmichael and Hamilton (9), Skolnick (32), Knowles and Prewitt (21), Yetman and Steele (44), Blauner (7), Jones (19), and Sanders (29).

The Emergence of the Institutional Racism Perspective

Although Carmichael and Hamilton apparently coined the term *institutional racism* and generated widespread interest in the relevance of this perspective as a model for examining white-nonwhite relations, some reference should be made to several individuals whose work indirectly laid a foundation for this approach (9).

As early as 1944 Myrdal discussed the deleterious effect of "institutional segregation," which was defined as *the segregation of Negroes in public facilities and private commercial establishments* (27, p. 627). The definition is limited, but this is understandable since the *American Dilemma* is primarily concerned with theoretical explanations of antiblack prejudice and the link of prejudice to legal segregation. Myrdal, nevertheless, offered an incisive description of the causal antecedents and effects of institutionalized segregation. Cox was one of the first to argue that economic forces should be fundamental considerations in discussing race relations (10). Although Cox devoted much of his attention to the *attitudes* that facilitated economic subordination of racial minorities, his holistic emphasis on economic exploitation implied the necessity of focusing on institutions. By describing the factors that functioned to create a pattern of extreme segregation and discrimination, the historian Woodward showed the importance of taking into account the historical interplay of political, economic, and legal forces (43). This shift in focus was also foreshadowed in studies seeking to explain intergroup relations within entire institutions (5; 16; 23).

The suggestion here is not that the above sources were necessarily instrumental in generating the conceptual framework now termed *institutional racism*, but only that as the position of blacks changed, so did the discipline's theoretical tools.

Basic Themes

There is considerable consensus regarding certain critical aspects of the institutional-racism perspective.

The Importance of History

While not unique to institutional-racism theorizing, there is a common emphasis on the importance of the deep roots and lasting effects of historical oppression. It is maintained that, historically, institutions defined and regulated norms, role relationships, and sanctions that were racially distinct.

The institutional-racism approach amplifies earlier descriptions of a minority's position in society by focusing on the mechanisms by which the majority has sustained its dominance. For example, several writers have discussed the importance of a racism ideology that, proclaiming racial superiority over another grouping, justified a differential allocation of privileges (19, pp. 8-14; 44, pp. 361-62; 21, pp. 7-14). The historically determined differential access to power and prestige has also been stressed as an important benefit derived and sustained by the dominant group (19, pp. 117-118; 9, pp. 6-16; 7, pp. 21-28). Writers have also emphasized that the historical structure of economic, educational, and political inequality are still reflected in the privileged position of whites presently (7, pp. 23-28; 21, chs. 2-4, 6; 9, ch. 1; 19, pp. 132-40). Although there is considerable variation in these discussions in terms of their comprehensiveness and documentation of the historical factors that have structured current racial relationships, there is agreement, nonetheless, that such historical components as a racist ideology, differential access to power and privilege, subordination within institutions, and restrictive laws have been crucial in shaping, legitimating, and maintaining a racially stratified society.

Individuals and Attitudes

Traditionally, models examining race relations have focused on prejudicial attitudes or some combination of attitudes and acts. Institutional racism has been interpreted as a dynamic process whose persistence and existence does not rely on prejudicial attitudes. Instead, institutional racism can occur without "conscious bigotry" (21, p. 5; 29, p. 28) and often has little direct reference to "attitudinal factors or the prejudices of majority group members" (44, p. 363). According to Skolnick (32, p. 180), institutional racism may even operate independently of individual prejudice: "A society in which most of the good jobs are held by one race, and the dirty jobs are held by people of another color, is a society in which racism is institutionalized no matter what the beliefs of its members are"; Jones argues, similarly, that institutional laws, customs, and practices may be racist "whether or not the individuals maintaining those practices have racist intentions" (19, p. 131).

Visibility and Intent

Most writers agree that in contrast to "individual" racism, institutional racism is often considerably less visible, more subtle, and less intentional. In drawing the distinction between individual and institutional racism, Carmichael and Hamilton point out that the latter is "less identifiable in terms of specific individuals" who may be committing overt and visible acts that cause injury or destruction (9, p. 4). Blauner agrees that the processes involved in institutional racism are often "nonintentional," compared to individual racism, which "tends to be more direct and volitional" (7, pp. 187-88). Jones suggests that negative consequences accrue within institutions because of the subtle and unintentional form of institutional racism and that such consequences "may be both unforeseen and undesirable by the responsible institutions" (19, p. 131). In distinguishing between individual and institutional racism, Knowles and Prewitt demonstrate the "invisibility" of the latter by pointing out the difficulties entailed in establishing culpability (21, p. 6). Sanders also refers to institutional racism as a "covert" and "subtle" process operating in the "established and respected forces of the society" (29, p. 28). Finally, even the United States Commission on Civil Rights has pointed to several structural factors, largely "unrecognized," "indirect," and "invisible," but which have resulted in institutional subordination (38, pp. 10-11).

Bureaucratic Functions

Another theme that is prevalent in the institutional-racism literature is that, once racist policies have been institutionalized, the role of bigoted individuals can be of relatively little importance because the *operating* bureaucratic policies, priorities, and regulations function to disqualify minority participation. According to Skolnick, "institutions have developed standards, procedures, and rigidities to inhibit the Negro's drive for equality" (32, p. 180). Since the established rules of bureaucracies have already prestructured a group's lack of alternatives, "the individual only has to conform to the operating norms of the organization and the institution will do the discriminating for him" (4, p. 143). Yetman and Steele point out that even if certain racially exclusive policies are modified within an institution (for example, changing admissions qualifications to universities), inequities in other institutions will continue to perpetuate inequality (for instance, the low quality of ghetto schools and the inability of black parents to pay college expenses) (44, p. 365). Blauner also emphasizes that a racist social structure is not maintained by prejudicial attitudes but by the institutionalization of racial inequality, so that "institutions either exclude or restrict the participation of racial groups by procedures that have become conventional, part of the bureaucratic system of rules and regulations" (7, pp. 9-10). Thus, it is the operation of a system of bureaucratic rules within institutions that is crucial for maintaining racial control.

Interaction and Accumulation of Inequality

Authors interested in institutional racism stress that since institutions are interrelated, racial control is reinforced across institutional sectors. Baron argues that this "web of racism" is characterized by white dominance and black subordination across institutional sectors (4, pp. 160-61). Much of Knowles and Prewitt's book is devoted to describing the comprehensiveness of the exclusion of blacks from such major institutions as the economy, education, law, and the polity (21). Discussing the lack of participation in the economy, Jones points out that missing out on the "first levels of economic viability" perpetuates other economic losses (19, pp. 132-35). For example, not having property means not being able to partake of other related benefits, such as tax advantages and resale profits.

Such inequity is also cumulative. This is one aspect that institutional-racism theorists are very clear about. The familiar argument here is that once a minority is excluded from one institution, chances are greater that it will also be excluded from other institutional privileges.

Consequences

The final theme apparent in institutional racism is that consequences are the most important indicator of the presence of institutional racism. For Yetman and Steele structural discrimination, by definition, refers to the "effects" of inequality (44, p. 363). Knowles and Prewitt state that one can demonstrate that a nation is racist when one can understand its racist policy, and that the racist policy "can be understood only when we are willing to take a look at the continuing and irrefutable racist consequences of the major institutions in American life" (21, pp. 13-14). Skolnick buttresses his argument that American universities are maintaining institutional racism by also pointing to the racially differential results (32, p. 100). Blauner underscores the juxtaposition between a white professor's actively renouncing institutional racism on the one hand and partaking of the consequences of institutional racism on the other (7, pp. 276-77). Such consequences include being a member of an all-white department in an all-white occupation in an all-white institution that serves an all-white neighborhood. Jones suggests, further, that obtaining evidence for institutional racism is much less problematic than proving the existence of prejudice since, "One need only look for gross racial inequities in the outcomes of institutional operations to level charges of institutional racism" (19, p. 116). Carmichael and Hamilton also rely almost exclusively on examples of consequences—for example, dilapidated slum tenements and high infant-mortality rates—in presenting their argument for the existence of institutional racism (9, p. 4).

Criticisms of the Perspective

Although some common themes have been developed by advocates of the institutional-racism perspective, there are a number of problems that should be discussed. Some problems are relatively minor. For example, although writers agree that institutional racism is considerably more subtle than "individual" racism, there is less agreement about the degree of visibility and intent. Thus, Carmichael and Hamilton point out that institutional racism differs from individual racism because the former is less overt in its perpetration of death or other destruction (9, p. 4). Blauner argues that the processes involved in institutional racism are "usually nonintentional" compared to individual racism that "tends to be more direct and volitional" (7, pp. 187-88). Jones, however, states that institutional racism can be either overt or covert, intentional or unintentional, and that both overt and covert forms of racism are usually intentional (19, p. 13). To close the circle, Knowles and Prewitt argue that both the individual acts of racism and racist institutional policy "may be masked intentionally or innocently" (21, p. 5).

Although such inconsistencies must be resolved, they are less serious than the following issues.

Definitions

One of the most glaring dilemmas is definitional ambiguity, or, in some cases, the absence of any attempts at defining institutional racism. An example of the latter situation is Knowles and Prewitt's description of some of the characteristics of institutional racism (namely, intentional or innocent, absence of conscious bigotry, not motivated by individuals) without a definition of exactly what is meant by the concept (21, pp. 4-6).

When definitions are attempted, theorists are faced with the difficult task of differentiating among institutional racism and other forms of exclusion. Several attempts have been made to resolve this problem. For example, Yetman and Steele delineate between discrimination that is motivated either by behavior or by attitudes (44, p. 363). Thus, for Yetman and Steele, "individual discrimination" and "institutionalized discrimination" are ultimately reducible to psychological attitudes—"either the actor is himself prejudiced or else he abdicates to the sanctions of a prejudiced reference group." Their "structural discrimination" (which appears equivalent to the notion of institutional racism) is not attributed directly to prejudice. Instead, structural discrimination "refers to the effects of inequalities that are rooted in the systemwide operation of a society and have little relation to attitudinal factors or the prejudices of majority group members" (44, p. 363). The major problem with the definitions of some analysts is that, outside of equating institutional racism with its consequences, there is little elaboration of the critical dimensions and operational mechanisms involved in the concept.

Another definitional ambiguity is the occasional tendency to both reject and accept the importance of attitudes in discussing institutional racism. Although Carmichael and Hamilton stress that institutional racism does not rely on bigoted individuals committing racially based injurious acts, they also state that it does rely "on the active and pervasive operation of antiblack attitudes and practices" (9, p. 5). Yet their subsequent treatment of institutional racism as being synonymous with colonialism illustrates that the authors are not primarily interested in attitudes. In a similar vein Sanders defines institutional racism as occurring without the presence of conscious bigotry, but he then proceeds to equate institutional racism with "institutional subordination," which refers to actions, institutional structures, or attitudes "[that] subordinate a person or group because of his or their color" (29, pp. 28-29). Such usages of institutional racism pose problems because they connote that institutional racism still depends on individuals who are discriminating because they are internalizing prejudicial attitudes.

There appear to be two major reasons for the definitional ambiguity. The first is that theorists are still exploring the uncertain boundaries and processes of institutional racism. That is, what type of inequality should be attributed to institutional racism? How should these unequal consequences be distinguished from the ones that accrue because of prejudice or discrimination of bigoted individuals?

The second difficulty is that since we are concerned with institutional racism, how can we indicate that we are talking about institutional racism and not simply racism within institutions? Yetman and Steele have partly avoided this conceptual overlap by defining racism as a composite of ideological and behavioral components, then focusing on the behavioral aspects of discrimination (44, pp. 360-63). Although structural discrimination is subsumed under racism, both the terminology and the definition suggest that there is conceptual and theoretical distinctiveness. Blauner, also, partially, succeeds in doing this. In his analysis Blauner utilizes a broad model of internal colonialism delineating four components of colonization, one of which is racism. According to Blauner, racism can be subjective—located in prejudice and other feelings— or objective—institutionalized and located in structured hierarchies (7, pp. 9-10). Blauner, however, neither develops these distinctions further nor does he clearly state whether objective racism is the same as institutional racism.

Unit of Analysis

Part of the reason for this conceptual ambiguity may be the overemphasis on racism and the neglect of institutions. This neglect is understandable, since the theory and research related to concrete institutional operations, particularly internal procedures, have been negligible. The lack of preexisting theory and data has lead to the situation of theorizing about the institutional level, but supporting discussions of institutional racism by utilizing illustrations from the individual or societal level.

One example of this contradictory approach is Jones's extension of Kovel's notion of "dominative" and "aversive" racists as a parallel to institutional racism. According to Jones, "Those white racists who correspond to the dominative types could be expected to create and perpetuate institutions whose racism corresponds to the overt character of the dominative racist" (19, p. 130). Such a comparison blurs the important distinction between individual prejudice and institutional racism by attributing structurally unequal consequences to intentional and prejudiced attitudes.

It seems that even when theorists acknowledge the theoretical importance of the institution rather than the individual as the unit of analysis, proposals for social policy and change still revert back to an individualistic focus. For example, Knowles and Prewitt represent one of the atypical situations in which some concern is expressed for understanding the functions of institutions before attempting an analysis of institutional racism (21, pp. 130-33). In the last analysis, however, the authors suggest getting together with "friends, fellow workers, and neighbors" to mobilize attacks against institutional racism. The point here is that although the theory is concerned with institutions, the theorists are still undecided about the role of the individual.

Methodology and Research

As discussed above, theorists generally cite evidence for the presence of institutional racism by pointing to consequences, rather than describing the mechanisms of institutional racism. Since the concept is still definitionally complex and elusive, there is as yet no clear theoretical direction for isolating the variables that should be examined and that would guide field-research efforts. Most of the information supporting the perspective of institutional racism has come not from research directed at analyzing institutional racism per se but from work that has been directed at examining the position of blacks in a variety of institutional settings (8; 36; 34; 13). Some of the writers working in the area of institutional racism have provided limited empirical data regarding the manifestations of institutional racism within individual institutions (21; 44; 7; 9), or devoted some space to discussions of the interrelationships among institutions (4; 19). For the most part, however, there has not been an attempt to combine both theory and research.

To our knowledge, there has been only one research attempt, to date, that has utilized the institutional-racism perspective as a framework for field research. Sanders states that since "specific documentation of institutional racism is nonexistent," the study would "compensate for the lack by presenting documentation and insights in this relatively virgin field in inquiry" (29, p. 16). Although Sanders defines institutional racism as an "act," one objective of the study is to explore the patterns of institutional racism as perceived by leaders in newly formed professional organizations. Sanders later describes fifteen indicators of institutional racism used in the study. One of these is "role and function" (29, pp. 48-52). Although Sanders conceptualizes this variable along structural lines, the operationalization is based on perceptions and attitudes. Thus, there seems to be an incongruence between the theory and the methodology. To study institutional racism it seems necessary to examine the operation of norms and roles within institutions. Yet the historically prescribed racial roles and blatantly racist attitudes that have established and structured these norms and roles have become largely defunct. The researcher is faced, then, with the dilemma of measuring processes and practices of exclusion that are not readily apparent.

A final criticism of the institutional-racism model might be that: 1) it is not clear whether the perspective presently applies only to racial or ethnic or to both types of minorities; 2) if it applies only to racial minorities, does it also explain the position of racial groups that are not black; and 3) if it applies only to blacks, how useful is its explanatory power? In addition, there is the question of its cross-cultural or cross-national relevance.

For the most part, writers seem to be applying the institutional-racism perspective to explain only the black situation. Although such terms as *minorities, racial groups,* and *subordinate groups* suggest the model's applicability to all minorities, there is minimal expository material presented on nonblack groups or ethnic minorities. The only exception to this ambivalence is Blauner's work, which clearly applies the notion of institutional racism to other minorities (7).

It is probably safe to state that writers have decided *only* that the model does apply to blacks. The criticism could be made, then, that theorists and researchers in this area should be concerned with such questions as the place (if any) of white ethnic groups, nonwhite groups, and, if the model is applied only to blacks, its relevance to both the North and the South and to other countries. In general, the institutional-racism perspective might be defended in terms of its immaturity. As the model develops, it is expected that many of these issues will be faced and examined.

Suggestions for Extending the Institutional Racism Perspective

Because of the general focus of the literature on the historical and contemporary position of black Americans, we are here limiting our revisionist suggestions to the black situation. We view the black situation as an important test case of the working model proposed here. If the exclusion of blacks in various institutional sectors can be satisfactorily explained by a well-developed institutional-racism perspective, its utility may then be extended to include other minorities such as Mexican Americans and Native Americans.

At this point in time there should be serious efforts directed not only at evaluating the state of the institutional-racism literature but also suggesting methodological guidelines for testing the theory.

Dimensions in Inequality

Consider Table 1 depicting the types of discriminatory practices that currently maintain racial inequality. This table does not purport to present an exhaustive compilation of the existing types of inequality. It does point out, however: 1) that inequality should be distinguished in terms of its source—behavior based on or independent of prejudice; 2) that, if behavioral components constitute the basic source of inequality, behavioral input can be further delineated according to purpose—deliberate or incidental; and 3) that inequality due to behavior not prejudically motivated can have several determinants, the most important of which is institutional racism. Thus, if we are concerned with institutional racism as one explanation of current racial stratification, this concept should not be used synonymously nor interchangeably with the other determinants of inequality.

Table 1

Types of Discriminatory Practices That Maintain Racial Inequality

Discriminatory practices that are motivated by prejudice		Discriminatory practices that are not motivated by prejudice
Discriminatory effect is deliberate	Discriminatory effect is incidental	Discriminatory effect is incidental
Type A	Type B	Type C
Prejudiced discrimination "Individual discrimination" (Yetman and Steele) "Individual racism" (Jones) "Aversive" "Dominative"	Conforming discrimination "Institutional discrimination (Yetman and Steele)	Institutional racism (for example, credentialism)

The manifestations of inequality will vary along such dimensions as visibility, degree of intensity, scope of effect on blacks, and level of analysis, depending on the type of inequality. That is, the inequality listed as Type A will, for the most part, be overt and emotionally intense. Merton's bigot (the "prejudiced discriminator"), Jones's individual racist, Kovel's dominative racist, and the individual discriminator of Yetman and Steele are all individuals who discriminate consciously because they are motivated by prejudice. However, such behavior has probably declined because of new legal constraints and shifting attitudes, although it can still affect the situations of individual blacks, or blacks in small or large groups. The causes of Type B inequality are less overt and obvious because the discriminating individual acquiesces in the prejudicial opinions, attitudes, or expectations of an important reference group. For example, the "unprejudiced discriminator" may hesitate to speak up against discrimination because he might lose status or be penalized by his prejudiced associates (26, p. 106); or the realtor may refuse to sell a home to a black because he is afraid of alienating his white customers. This is the type of discrimination Yetman and Steele refer to as "institutionalized discrimination," one of the more confusing terms in this general literature. Type B inequality, although a by-product of reference-group prejudice, may affect larger numbers than Type A. The causes of Type C inequality are far less obvious, but are crucial in excluding large numbers of blacks from equal participation in legal, economic, and political institutions. The set of institutionalized practices and procedures lying behind Type C inequality is what most authors have in mind, at least to a significant degree, when they delineate a concept of institutional racism.

Summarizing our previous analysis, we suggest the following working definition of institutional racism for further research:

Institutional racism refers to the structure of inequality: 1) reflected in the racially based differential allocation of status, privileges, and material rewards in numerous institutional sectors; and 2) shaped by the historically precipitated and currently persisting process of subordination whose mechanisms primarily involve the routine imposition of conventional norms by often unprejudiced role players in the various institutional sectors in a way that, though covert and usually unintentional, produces racially relevant consequences.

These effects can be cumulative within and across institutions, resulting in the exclusion of very large groups of blacks from certain areas in most institutions and the long-term domination of whites in the social system. For example, "credentialism" here refers to a general process functioning within institutional racism. That is, credentialism is a procedure by which blacks are disqualified from competition because they fail to meet universalistic, objectively formulated standards. A commonly cited example is that of admissions policies in universities. For example, students must have certain grade-point averages and college-entrance-examination test scores. These qualifications are evaluated impersonally by college officials according to objective admissions standards that function to intentionally and rationally exclude *all* potential students who are not qualified. Racial exclusion is perpetuated because many of these rules and policies were originally set up by, and with the intention of serving the needs of, a specific stratum of society—the white middle class. The routine imposition of similar universalistic criteria can limit black entry into certain economic institutions or stall blacks in a strategic stage of employment progression.

A Critical Distinction

Our model of institutional racism has two major conceptual components: 1) modes of operation—norms and their application by critical personnel who limit black access to resources within any one institution; and 2) consequences—the operation of norms and roles within and cumulatively across institutions provides a basic system of control over access to resources, excluding and under-representing large proportions of blacks from the labor market, polity, welfare structures, educational processes, and the housing market.

As Table 2 illustrates, institutional racism is comprised of at least two essential components—modes of operation and consequences—that should be considered in research and theoretical development. First, there must be a concern for discovering the mechanisms of institutional racism. That is, which norms and how roles have been operating to limit black participation within an institution. In the area of norms, for example, formal laws, bureaucratic regulations, and rules of allocation and decisions regarding the distribution of goods and services might be systematically examined, from the inside, in all major institutional areas. In the area of roles, such issues as power relations, expectations for role performance, the behavior of critical personnel who apply norms and the channels of communication between role specialists would become critical for systematic investigation.

The consequences of institutional racism refer to the representation and participation of blacks within one institutional area. Black participation should be examined not only at specific points within an institution (for instance, ghetto schools), but traced through one institution at all levels as well. That is, if blacks fail to qualify for col-lege-entrance requirements, the explanations for this failure lie in a number of obstacles that blacks must overcome in their progression through a number of educational organizations. The consequences of institutional racism do not refer to the situation of individual blacks, but to blacks in general. While we are studying the operations and consequences of institutional racism, it is important to remember that inequality in only one organization does not necessarily indicate institutional racism.

Since institutional racism, in its broadest sense, refers to inequality

TABLE 2: OPERATIONS AND CONSEQUENCES OF INSTITUTIONAL RACISM WITHIN THREE MAJOR INSTITUTIONAL AREAS: EDUCATION, THE ECONOMY, THE POLITY

Educational Institution	Economic Institutions	Political Institutions

1. Ghetto schools
   a. teacher shortages
   b. low expenditure per pupil
   c. large classrooms
   d. white control of school board
2. Inadequate preparation for higher education
   a. limited curricula
   b. inadequate facilities and educational materials
   c. low performance expectations by faculty and administration
3. Disqualification in college admission requirements
	1. White ownership of enterprise
	2. Employment
	   Hiring practices
	   a. employers can impose high educational standards
	   b. application of subtle criteria by employers (e.g. speech and deportment)
	   c. limited recruitment channels
	   d. concentration of blacks in marginal or declining firms
	
	   Promotion systems
	   a. occupational ceilings
	   b. specific job classifications
	   c. specific production units
	   d. restriction to low-paying job classifications
	3. Labor union participation
	   a. restrictive apprenticeship programs
	   b. membership in unskilled positions
	4. Consumer exploitation
		1. Political participation
		   a. low voter registration rates
		   b. gerrymandering
		   c. restrictive electoral systems
		2. Office-holding
		   a. limited largely to local offices
		   b. lack of representation in local government
		   c. positions in non-decision making offices
		   d. lack of wealth to influence political decisions

Disparity in black-white achievement on all educational levels	Disparity in black-white economic attainment in all spheres of the economy	Disparity in black-white power within the polity

that is due to a cumulative process within and across all or most important institutional areas, these interrelationships should be examined in a comprehensive analysis. Conceptually, the extremely complex interdependence between institutions in terms of black access to resources might be diagrammed as seen in Table 3. The

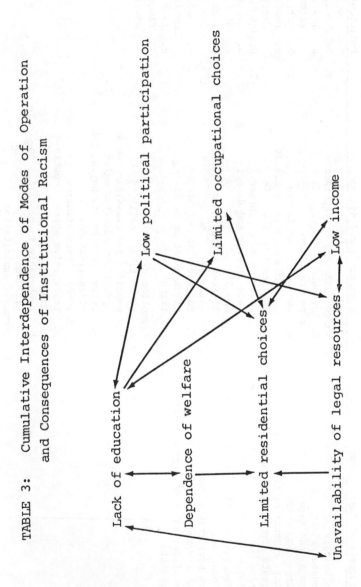

TABLE 3: Cumulative Interdependence of Modes of Operation and Consequences of Institutional Racism

notion of the cumulative and interrelated impact of institutional operations and consequences is important in describing institutional racism for several reasons. First, since blacks were subordinated in one crucial institutional area—the economy—there has been an inertia problem in the sense that blacks have difficulty in "catching up" within this institutional sector. Moreover, this inertia has affected black quality in other institutions, so that black exclusion from any one institution also established preconditions for inequality in other institutions.

Application of the Model

How this model might be applied to the study of institutional racism can be *briefly* illustrated in the following discussion of the jury-selection process.

Sociohistorical Factors of Subordination

Between 1619 and 1865 the legal status of blacks paralleled their general position in the social system—slaves were generally without legal rights. In courtrooms, neither slaves nor free blacks could testify against whites; slaves were considered competent witnesses only when testifying against another slave or free black; and, in criminal cases, when a slave was tried, the jurors had to be slaveholders (33, pp. 206-224). Between 1865-1920 racial inequality was sanctioned through Supreme Court decisions and state and federal laws. During this period blacks were excluded from jury service through various disenfranchising laws. As a result of the new voting requirements, by the turn of the century both the number of black voters and the numbers of black jurors had dwindled to insignificant proportions. Since World War II black participation on juries has been restricted primarily because black voter registration (the basic source of juror names in many states) has met resistance through coercion, intimidation, voter purges, exclusion of black voters from crucial political meetings, and omissions of registered black voters from voting lists. Most recently, blacks have not been serving on juries in reasonable numbers— not primarily because there have been overwhelming legal restrictions, or harassment due to prejudice—but because blacks have been unable to meet objective statutory qualifications.

Operation of Subordination

In the case of jury selection, legal norms and legal social-control agents function to qualify or disqualify prospective jurors for service. The norms consist in most cases of written rules that are impersonal and applied uniformly to all potential jurors. These rules prescribe and proscribe the behavior and duties of jury commissioners (or district clerks), judges, and attorneys during four stages of the selection process.

Stage 1: Master Jury List

To qualify as a prospective juror in many states an individual should, for example, be able to read, write, and speak English, be a resident of the state and county for a specified length of time, be twenty-one-years old, be a registered voter, and have no previous criminal convictions. Even before the lists of names reach the clerk or commissioner, many blacks will have been unable to meet these requirements because of their position within other institutional spheres. For example, dropping out of a poor-quality ghetto school will impair the reading and writing skills of blacks and disqualify them as "illiterate." Since in many areas the poorly educated are also more likely to be uninformed about the critical importance of voter registration, many will not be registered voters. Because blacks are underemployed and highly mobile seeking jobs, they will often not be able to meet state and county requirements. Since blacks are more likely than whites to have been arrested and convicted, a criminal record will serve as a disqualifying factor.

The personnel who are responsible for screening individuals in terms of these requirements are usually white. However, their potential prejudices can have minimal impact during this state of the selection process, because blacks have already been disqualified through a series of objective and impersonal regulations.

Stage 2: Excuses and Exemptions

Exemption consists of being barred from jury service, regardless of desire to serve, because the "public interest" requires the individual to remain at his job (for instance, policemen, firemen, soldiers, or public officers). Since many states exempt women with young children or individuals who are in such professions as education and medicine, large numbers of black women are automatically excluded from service. Excused persons are people who are eligible for jury duty but may plea undue hardship or extreme inconvenience, which low-paid jury service would necessarily entail.

There are many individuals who ask to be excused simply to avoid jury duty for a variety of reasons. In the case of blacks, however, many of these reasons have been predetermined by the blacks' position in other institutions. For example, blacks may plead economic hardship because they are employed in jobs where employers are not sympathetic to "civic-responsibility" obligations. But then if employers encouraged blacks to serve, jury-duty remuneration is too low to justify a loss of wages. Also, black women who may be dependent on welfare, have preschool children, and who live in ghettos some distance from the courthouse, do not have the monetary means for child-care or transportation facilities to participate in jury duty. Poor health and high geographic mobility further deter the participation of potential black jurors. Since judges routinely excuse anyone who does not wish to serve, the potential prejudicial attitudes or individual discrimination by judges are largely neutralized, since some blacks seek disqualification for economic reasons or are eliminated because of the incidental impact of other institutions.

Stage 3: Panel and Voir Dire Examination

Unlike the previous stages, attorneys are not guided by written rules during their examination of the jury panel. Instead, over the years attorneys have formulated various "theories" about "good jurors" based on a number of demographic and attitudinal criteria. For example, in criminal cases affecting minorities such as blacks, the prosecution often does not want militant college students who might sympathize with a defendant, while the defense does not want businessmen or retired military personnel who are expected to be hostile toward most defendants. In civil cases, because "poor people are free with other peoples' money," they will be struck or retained by either side. In most cases, then, attorneys do have very strong beliefs about various segments of the population, including Catholics, women, businessmen, and even grandmothers. These definitions are evoked not just because attorneys are unleashing their personal stereotypes, but especially because such theories over the long run help attorneys eliminate the categories of individuals who are least likely to help them win a case.

This is not to say that there is absolutely no subjectivity or prejudice revealed by the critical actors in the jury-selection process; ethnocentric lawyers can strike minorities on strictly racial beliefs, disregarding the potential harm to a client. In such instances a few blacks may be excluded because of behavior motivated by prejudice. In most cases, however, such attitudes will not have to be evoked because black participation will have been already limited by the mechanisms of institutional racism (Stages 1 and 2 above).

Results

Even though most criminal defendants are black, by the time the filtering processes have terminated, the box of twelve jurors will usually be made up of eleven white, middle-class "good men" who are supposed to represent a "trial by peers" from a "cross section" of the community. Thus, even though half of the county may be comprised of blacks, the percentage of blacks who actually serve on the jury may be infinitesimal, even though prejudice or behavior based on prejudice may have had little direct effect on the outcome.

Conclusion

The general inaccessibility of data and the heretofore unavailability of a sound theory should not discourage organized-research endeavors to investigate the workings of institutions and their subordination of nonwhites. Several sources provide useful elaborations of the internal mechanisms of institutions that would be helpful in guiding institutional-racism research.

A potentially useful example of the type of research that might be used to describe how institutional racism is maintained is Doeringer and Piore's analysis of racial discrimination in internal labor markets (14). These authors point out some very specific mechanisms that function to deny black promotion within the labor market. Some of these measures include the restriction of blacks to lower-paying classifications, limitations placed on black mobility "on the white progression leader," and separation of blacks into job units that are unrelated to promotion in other jobs. Doeringer and Piore further specify how such exclusionary tactics have a cumulative effect in reducing the economic opportunities of blacks to compete with whites for present and future promotions (14).

Whether or not institutional racism will make a real theoretical contribution to the study of race relations remains to be seen. Its main contribution lies in its probable impact on our overall understanding of the dynamic forces functioning to maintain racially superordinate-subordinate relationships in American society.

To summarize, this chapter has suggested that the institutional-racism perspective is important in suggesting key objectives for research—a focus on institutions, rather than groups or individuals; a systematic study of the norms, roles, and statuses that are responsible for structuring institutions, an emphasis on historical groundings; a delineation of the interrelatedness of institutional functions; and an emphasis on the cumulative effects of racial inequality. Some typological schemes were also presented suggesting the consideration of such factors as the mechanisms, intent, and unit of analysis in discussions of institutional racism. If institutional-racism research could be conducted according to a carefully developed theoretical formulation, this perspective would make a major contribution not only to our understanding of racial inequality, but would also provide far-reaching social-policy implications.

References

1. Adorno, T. W.; Frankel-Brunswick, Else; Levinson, Daniel J.; and Sanford, H. Nevitt. 1950. *The Authoritarian Personality*. New York: Harper and Row.
2. Allport, Gordon W. 1954. *The Nature of Prejudice*. Reading, Mass.: Addison-Wesley.
3. Antonovsky, Aaron. 1960. "The Social Meaning of Discrimination." *Phylon*, pp. 81-95.
4. Baron, Harold M. 1969. "The Web of Urban Racism." In *Institutional Racism in America*. Edited by Louis L. Knowles and Kenneth Prewitt. Englewood Cliffs, N.J.: Prentice-Hall, pp. 134-76.
5. Becker, Gary. 1957. *The Economics of Discrimination*. Chicago: University of Chicago Press.
6. Blalock, Hubert M., Jr. 1967. *Toward a Theory of Minority-Group Relations*. New York: Wiley.
7. Blauner, Robert. 1972. *Racial Oppression in America*. New York: Harper and Row.
8. Bloch, Herman D. 1969. *The Circle of Discrimination: An Economic and Social Study of the Black Man in New York*. New York: New York University Press.
9. Carmichael, Stokely, and Hamilton, Charles. 1967. *Black Power: The Politics of Liberation in America*. New York: Random House/Vintage Books.
10. Cox, Oliver Cromwell. 1948. *Caste, Class, and Race: A Study in Social Dynamics*. New York: Doubleday.

11. Davis, Allison, and Dollard, John. 1940. *Children of Bondage.* Washington, D.C.: American Council on Education.
12. Davis, Allison; Gardner, Burleigh B.; and Gardner, Mary R. 1941. *Deep South.* Chicago: University of Chicago Press.
13. Denton, John H. 1967. *Apartheid American Style.* Berkeley, Calif.: Diablo Press.
14. Doeringer, Peter B., and Piore, Michael J. 1971. *Internal Labor Markets and Manpower Analysis.* Lexington, Mass.: Heath-Lexington Books.
15. Glazer, Nathan, and Moynihan, Daniel P. 1963. *Beyond the Melting Pot: The Negroes, Puerto Ricans, Italians, and Irish of New York City.* Cambridge, Mass.: MIT Press.
16. Greenberg, Jack. 1959. *Race Relations and American Law.* New York: Columbia University Press.
17. Hamblin, Robert L. 1962. "The Dynamics of Racial Discrimination." *Social Problems* 10 (Fall): 103-120.
18. Hartley, E. L. 1946. *Problems in Prejudice.* New York: Kings Crown Press.
19. Jones, James M. 1972. *Prejudice and Racism.* Reading, Mass.: Addison-Wesley.
20. Killian, Lewis, and Grigg, Charles. 1964. *Racial Crisis in America: Leadership in Conflict.* Englewood Cliffs, N.J.: Prentice-Hall.
21. Knowles, Louis L., and Prewitt, Kenneth, eds. 1969. *Institutional Racism in America.* Englewood Cliffs, N.J.: Prentice-Hall.
22. Kovel, Joe. 1970. *White Racism: A Psychohistory.* New York: Pantheon.
23. Laurenti, Luigi. 1960. *Property Values and Race.* Berkeley, Cal.: University of California Press.
24. Mangum, Charles S., Jr. 1940. *The Legal Status of the Negro.* Chapel Hill, N.C.: University of North Carolina Press.
25. Marden, Charles F., and Meyer, Gladys. 1952. *Minorities in American Society.* New York: Litton Educational Publishing.
26. Merton, Robert K. 1949. "Discrimination and the American Creed." In *Discrimination and National Welfare.* Edited by R. M. MacIver. New York: Harper and Brothers, pp. 99-126.
27. Myrdal, Gunnar. 1944. *An American Dilemma: The Negro Problem and Modern Democracy.* New York: Harper and Brothers.
28. Park, Robert E. 1950. *Race and Culture.* Glencoe, Ill.: Free Press.
29. Sanders, Charles L. 1972. *Black Professionals' Perceptions of Institutional Racism in Health and Welfare Organizations.* Fair Lawn, N.J.: R. E. Burdick.
30. Schermerhorn, R. A. 1970. *Comparative Ethnic Relations: A Framework for Theory and Research.* New York: Random House.
31. Simpson, George E., and Yinger, J. Milton. 1953. *Racial and Cultural Minorities: An Analysis of Prejudice and Discrimination.* New York: Harper and Brothers.

32. Skolnick, Jerome H. 1969. *The Politics of Protest.* New York: Ballantine Books.
33. Stampp, Kenneth, M. 1956. *The Peculiar Institution: Slavery in the Antebellum South.* New York: Knopf.
34. Stone, Chuck. 1968. *Black Political Power in America.* New York: Dell.
35. Strong, Donald S. 1968. *Negroes, Ballots, and Judges: National Voting Rights Legislation in the Federal Courts.* University, Ala.: University of Alabama Press.
36. Tabb, William K. 1970. *The Political Economy of the Black Ghetto.* New York: Norton.
37. Tannenbaum, Frank. 1946. *Slave and Citizen: The Negro in the Americas.* New York: Random House/Vintage Books.
38. United States Commission on Civil Rights. 1970. *Racism in America and How to Combat It.* Washington, D.C.: U.S. Government Printing Office.
39. van den Berghe, Pierre L. 1967. *Race and Racism: A Comparative Perspective.* New York: Wiley.
40. Vander Zanden, James W. 1963. *American Minority Relations.* New York: Ronald Press.
41. Wagley, Charles, and Harris, Marvin. 1958. *Minorities in the New World: Six Case Studies.* New York: Columbia University Press.
42. Wirth, Louis. 1928. *The Ghetto.* Chicago: University of Chicago Press.
43. Woodward, C. Vann. 1955. *The Strange Career of Jim Crow.* New York: Oxford University Press.
44. Yetman, Norman R., and Steele, C. Hoy, eds. 1971. *Majority and Minority: The Dynamics of Racial Ethnic Relations.* Boston: Allyn and Bacon.

II

Strategies for Institutional Change

Community Development
Self-determination
Participation as a
Human Right
Political Action and Reaction
Flexible Methodology

Overview

Homeostasis or the need to maintain a steady state in society has caught the imagination of most social scientists. Few study the significance of homeokinesis, the need to maintain continuous change in society. Homeostasis and homeokinesis are complementary, not contradictory functions. Yet sociological imagination has been more concerned with stability and less concerned with change.

More effort has been directed to understanding social structure. Social scientists have a good deal to say about social control but know less about innovation and change. Probably there is an ideological basis for this emphasis. Social scientists appear to value tradition over innovation. For this reason, they have placed their research skills at the service of the established people of power and have tended to ignore the needs of the poor and oppressed. The chapter on "Community Development and Social Change" indicates that even social scientists who have studied change have overlooked the actions of the insurgents.

The renewed interest in race relations could overcome this limitation in perspective, for it is becoming increasingly clear in race relations today that the process of interaction among black, brown, and white people is as important as the structured outcomes. This is another way of saying, "the medium is the message."

While the poor and oppressed cannot implement community

programs for their own benefit if they require resources greater than their personal means, they can affect the course of social history through their veto action. They can upset stability and disrupt the equilibrium. They can refuse to honor tradition. Veto action is a kind of social power that sociologists have not studied adequately.

Conflict, compromise, and cooperation are all aspects of the social system. Cooperation is a process of social action that contributes to stability, and conflict is a process of social action that contributes to change. It is important to understand the full range of the social process, as a study of community development reveals.

The community-development model for social change involves: (1) self-determination (that is, the poor and oppressed or sub-dominant power groups identify for themselves action priorities); (2) the conscious use of conflict (for the purpose of creating so much discomfort in the social system that the dominant people of power will change—the price they must pay for a new equilibrium and a period of stability); (3) goals that are rhetorically identified as human rights (and, therefore, are not as susceptible to negotiation as are privileges); and (4) compromise. Meyer Weinberg comments upon these components of the community-development model with reference to education. In the chapter on "A Historical Framework for Multi-cultural Education," Weinberg shows, by way of historical analysis, that our society never responded to the call to end inequality in education until the minorities demanded that the society respond. Before these demands were made, the dominant people of power set their own priorities. When the subdominants took the definition of their future into their own hands, they identified equality of educational opportunity as a human right. Issues of racial assimilation were ranked as less important in the hierarchy of priorities of minorities, although this appeared to be a major concern of members of the majority-group population. Weinberg's forecast for the future is that minorities will be what they themselves decide, and he urges the schools to create the instructional materials to achieve these ends.

The activities of insurgents in the political system are probably the most visible examples of successful community development. Edward Greer has written a most interesting chapter on black insurgency in Gary—"The 'Liberation' of Gary, Indiana." He describes how power was wrested from the traditional holders, the methods by which they attempted to remain in charge, and the inevitable compromises that are necessary between the new and old people of power.

The compromise process is troublesome. The insurgents are new members of the establishment. They need advice and consultation on how to run the machinery of government. The most readily available source of this knowledge is among those people who were recently displaced. A promise to continue some aspects of the old social structure is the price insurgents often pay to win the cooperation of the deposed. To do this, the insurgents must compromise. Their supporters interpret such moves as sell-outs. Compromise is indeed a hazardous process, necessary and essential, but dangerous and difficult. The community-development movement has not mastered this stage very well. It is the reason for much misunderstanding.

Not only will the deposed people of power effectively bargain for compromises, but they will eventually become a countervailing force for the purpose of regaining control as well. This principle is clearly indicated in the Jacksonville, Florida story as told by Lee Sloan and Robert M. French in their chapter on "Black Rule in the Urban South?" Good government was the slogan under which whites launched a movement to consolidate city and county governments, as the numbers of blacks in Jacksonville increased and as the numbers of whites declined. The surrounding Duval County was populated predominantly with whites; they controlled the county but wanted to retain city power, too. So they launched a consolidation campaign and won. This is a classic example of how the concentration of power in one center will tend to stimulate countervailing centers. An open and vital community is one in which community power relations are in a continuous state of flux.

Such flexibility is healthy. Homeostasis without homeokinesis results in stability and eventually rigidity. Different approaches are needed to contribute to community stability and change and to cope with contingency and the unanticipated. The chapter on "Methods Used by Blacks to Negotiate White Institutions" illustrates three kinds of adaptations that persons may make to social forces that disturb the emotions and thoughts. One may cooperate, withdraw, or become aggressive. The important thing is to use the appropriate adaptation under the appropriate set of circumstances. It is important to recognize that the use of one mode of adaptation in a situation that calls for another mode could result in failure. Although racism is a constant experience in this nation-state, no single method of response will always be effective in transcending or transforming oppression. Flexibility in approach is needed and most minorities use a variety of methods to cope with their racist environments.

Yet restricted practices that should be cause for concern are increasingly evident. Some racial minorities are stereotyping their response to the persisting racism in society. They are tending to withdraw from whites as an adaptive response to insult and injury. If this method of adaptation is used over a prolonged period of time as the only way of dealing with unpleasant interracial encounters, it could take on a life of its own independent of the stimulus of racism that initially provoked it and it could seek to perpetuate a community of like-minded and look-alike people. The institutionalization of a single method of adaptation could become an inappropriate response and eventually fail to relieve the suffering it originally was intended to relieve. Flexibility is freedom to change according to the requirements of the situation. Cooperation and aggressiveness as well as withdrawal are flexible adaptations. They are options, all of which should be retained.

9

Community Development
and Social Change

Charles V. Willie

The community-development literature in sociology is under-developed. One suspects that omissions in this field are due largely to the fact that many contemporary social scientists have been handmaidens of and apologists for the establishment.

In his book, *Maximum Feasible Misunderstanding*, Daniel Patrick Moynihan discusses the so-called war on poverty of the Johnson administration as if it were concocted out of the minds of university professors and as if the main issue was a hassle between the Columbia University and the Harvard University professors about the appropriate way to fight the war. According to Moynihan, the Columbia professors won and thus the war on poverty was lost (5). Although subtitled, "Community Action in the War on Poverty," Moynihan's book has not a single reference to the Rev. Martin Luther King, Jr. It is as if King's demonstrations were of no effect. This, of course, is not true. But the establishment-oriented writers of contemporary social science act as if the public policy-making is not affected by the action from below—the community-development movement.

Marshall Clinard has stated that "reports on urban developments . . .[throughout] the world have suggested that effective relations between politicians and citizens self-help projects are generally difficult" (3, pp. 275-76). Maybe this is why the politicians and the

151

professors, when they write about each other, ignore these unpleasant experiences that intrude into the social system and require a redefinition of operating procedures.

Clinard, for example, accepts the idea set forth by Carl Feiss that the basic weakness of slum programs is that slum people have not been storming city hall. Yet he does not see the storm after it begins. Clinard's book discounted protest by the average, American, black-slum dweller as doing anything for himself. From Clinard's perspective, self-help among black-slum dwellers in America should be defined as "self-initiated changes in [their] norms and values . . .relating to delinquency and crime, violence, illegitimacy, drug addiction, lack of family responsibility, and apathy toward educational opportunities." It is clear that Clinard prefers self-help programs that have impact on the disadvantaged and that are not designed to change the social system and the dominant people of power who generate and perpetuate disadvantaged circumstances (3, p. 311).

Demonstrations led by the Southern Christian Leadership Conference were part of a protest and self-help movement that was directed at the dominant people of power, rather than toward the disadvantaged as suggested by Clinard. Because there is little understanding of this kind of movement, Martin Luther King, Jr. also escaped the bibliography in Clinard's book about community development. It is interesting to note that the courageous community-development activities of King that were designed to change the established systems of oppression in America were recognized internationally but ignored in books about community development and community action authored by American social scientists at elite universities.

Another example of sociology written for members of the establishment is revealed in the limited perspective on community power that was published in a book on the sociology of education. The author, Wilbur B. Brookover, states that "every community has a power system. . . .There are people or groups in every community who make important decisions and have the ability to enforce them. . . .One cannot understand a community until he is able to locate the sources of power. . . .Decisions affecting the entire community may be made under informal circumstances at a poker game, luncheon, or party. . . .School people need to know the sources of power and need to have the support of the dominant power groups in the community if the school program is to function smoothly (2, pp. 378-79). Yet, James Allen, Jr., former Commissioner of Education for the State of New York, credited the new initiatives taken by school boards throughout the country to achieve quality education for all to the pressure from below, from community subdominants. He testified that "Negroes in their demonstrations, in their peaceful demonstrations, have done more than any other segment of our society to push us to the point, where we have now gone" (1, p. 207).

If a balanced framework, gradual evolution, or a smoothly functioning program is the goal of individuals who say that they support social change, then protest activity by the disadvantaged is ignored as it has been by several social scientists studying community development and community action. The continuation of such omissions is bad social science that no longer should be tolerated if a comprehensive understanding of social organization and change is one of the goals of scientific research.

Actually subdominant people are a great source for social change in all institutions in any society. They make their contributions to change through the community-development movement, which is the primary way that change in behalf of the poor and oppressed is initiated.

Following the riots in Los Angeles, New York City, Detroit, and other great cities, George Gallup sent his pollsters into black and white communities to discover what could be done to prevent civil disorders in central city ghettos. White dominant people of power listed better law enforcement as the number one priority, while black subdominant people of power said the provision of more and better jobs was the best way to prevent riots. Despite the fact that most riots occur in black ghettos, the nation acted upon the white priority, ignored the voices of the disadvantaged or subdominant people, and began teaching the National Guard and the Army better techniques of riot control. Not only did the nation act upon the white priority, it summarily rejected the number one black priority, which was jobs.

George Gallup published his findings in August of 1967. By January of 1968, the president had made up his mind to ask the Office of Economic Opportunity to reserve only $35 million to pay for emergency operations for the approaching summer. Congress passed $75 million to finance summer programs in 1967. The New York Times called this reduction in funds for antipoverty programs a "squeeze on the poor." Indeed it was a squeeze; for in July of 1968, the Associated Press reported that "summer jobs for slum youngsters. . .[in New York City] were cut from 43,000 [the previous year] to 25,000 for lack of funds to finance them."

Consider this sequence of actions and how the dominant people of power continue to ignore the priorities of subdominants. One year after the riots and one year after the people who engaged in the riots said that more and better jobs were ways of preventing further riots, the dominant people of power ignored or rejected their analysis. Jobs were decreased and police power was increased. What, then, was there for poor and oppressed people to do? They protested. The protest was a self-help move as subsequent actions proved.

Wednesday, 10 July 1968, one thousand five hundred youth demonstrated at city hall in New York City. They were demanding more summer jobs. The mayor was annoyed by the behavior of the demonstrators. He said it was disgraceful. The day following the demonstration, however, the Associated Press reported that the mayor dug into the city's empty purse and came up with enough money to finance at least 10,000 more jobs for youngsters in poor families.

The city and federal governments did not act earlier upon the request of black and poor people for more and better jobs until a protest community-action movement was launched. Their request was published and made known in the Gallup poll following the riots. But the city and federal governments ignored or rejected their request. By not acting upon the priority of poor and black people, the city and federal governments were inviting demonstrations and protests that came like thunder and lightning at city hall during the following summer. The poor and the oppressed had to force their priorities upon the community that ignored the findings of the Gallup poll.

One conclusion that should be readily apparent from this case is that all people have power, dominants as well as subdominants; however, only dominants have the power to implement community programs that require the resources that they may control. But subdominants as well as dominants have veto power. Elsewhere in an analysis of community development and the public schools, I pointed out that the veto power of subdominants is not invoked often and that many, therefore, fail to realize that it exists. "Thus, school superintendents and other public officials are surprised when their plans run aground due to veto actions of subdominants." I further pointed out that "because it is unanticipated and comes from an unexpected source, the veto power of subdominants is considered to be disruptive. . ." (7, p. 224).

Community development is a process of getting the people in the community to take action in their own behalf, based on goals of their own choosing. Political action is one important end result of community development. Each person benefits as a result of collective effort. He or she benefits in personal and concrete ways, such as obtaining more food, higher wages, better housing, or improved public services. The purpose of community development is to take action that will change the circumstances of individuals. Community development is organizing people into powerful groups for the purpose of getting the political machine to do that which it will not do unless pressured into acting. Community development is helping people to organize and make decisions about their own destiny. Community development is concerned with institutional change. In community development, the people choose their own representatives to negotiate major issues with the society at large. They are not selected by the establishment.

The dominant people of power have difficulty dealing with community development and the demands of subdominants. The dominant people are reluctant to share their power. They will not deal with subdominants on the terms of subdominants. Dominants want to act on their own list of priorities that may not be the priorities of the subdominant people. As long as dominant people of power continue to deal on their own terms with the sub-dominants—be they young people, poor people, or black and brown people—fuel will continue to be added to the protest movement. Community conflict will escalate.

Several social scientists—for example, Jay Schulman and Ward H. Goodenough—have concluded that conflict is inevitable in community development. Goodenough (in a personal communication) describes one goal of community development as a "search for self-respect." He goes on to say that "[community-] development efforts that acknowledge the legitimacy of this goal are more likely to be distressing to many influential persons in the dominant sector." In community development, Schulman has stated (in a personal communication) that "issues must be drawn that are specific. . .[and that have] direct and immediate payoff to the poor." He further stated that "there must be a commitment to the use of conflict tactics and an eagerness to engage in direct confrontation with authority holders."

The community-development movement recognizes the existence of incompatible desires among the people in a pluralistic society. Conflict then is a legitimate process by which a community attempts to accommodate the many different desires of its members. The major issue is how to deal with the inevitable conflict in community

development in a controlled nonviolent way that enhances everyone—
the dominants and the subdominants.

For a few years during the early seventies, I served as a member
of the Regional Health Advisory Committee for Region II of the
Department of Health, Education, and Welfare. We explored ways
of helping regional, comprehensive health-planning agencies become
more effective. I was chairman of a subcommittee that studied
the representation of the poor and minority groups in health-planning
agencies. We drafted a position paper that the entire committee
endorsed and issued. The paper was entitled, "Why and How to
Involve People of Disadvantaged Circumstances in Governing Boards
of Comprehensive Health Planning Agencies," and it made the
following points:

1. That a free society remains free only when there is continuous
   participation of the governed in the instruments and institutions
   of government, including official and voluntary agencies;
2. That a community should be involved in selecting its own
   representatives and that representatives should have sufficient
   knowledge of, loyalty to, and links with a locality to adequately
   make known the needs, interests, and way of life of a
   constituency;
3. That it is beneficial for a policymaking board to have a fine
   mixture of members with local loyalties and members who
   represent special-interest groups as well as unaffiliated members at large;
4. That such a decision-making group that is truly representative
   may experience tension, but that such tension usually is
   creative with deliberations among representatives of different
   special-interest groups serving as a self-correcting device for
   the organization;
5. That representatives of disadvantaged populations ought to be
   present in numbers sufficient to have an impact upon deliberations beyond that of token participation and that such representation should be not less than one-fifth of all board positions as the "critical mass" necessary for a significant effect
   upon decision making;
6. And finally, that policies and plans that promote the public
   interest are likely to be those policies and plans that are
   forged on the anvil of controversy by competing interest
   groups and that it is more appropriate to encounter controversy around the conference table where it can be dealt
   with in a controlled way, where bargaining, trade-offs, and
   compromises can be worked out.

In general, we tried to say that disadvantaged people who are members of a board must be looked upon as partners who have an equal say about what is and what ought to be, just as any other board member. We, of course, shall not bring about this state of affairs until our governing boards and bodies of all of our community organizations and agencies are heterogeneous, consisting of representatives of the various economic, age, ethnic, and racial populations in the community—we shall not set out to deliberately bring about this kind of participation, unless we genuinely believe in being orderly in a lawful way where laws and regulations that protect and punish derive from all the people and apply equally to all of the people. We shall not create truly democratic and diversified decision-making structures until older people, affluent people, and white people can acknowledge that they do not always know what is best for the young, the poor, and the blacks.

In a seminar on planning and evaluation at the Laboratory of Community Psychiatry of the Harvard Medical School a specialist in community psychiatry said that the most rapid way to bring about change in an organization is to give it new clients. In responding to the demands of a different clientele, a system necessarily must change or cease to exist. The psychiatrist further suggested that an organization could contribute to orderly change by deliberately introducing within itself dissident interests to which the total system must respond.

The idea of deliberately bringing dissident elements into a system as a way of contributing to planned social change (as opposed to revolutionary action) is not new. Vilfredo Paredo, the Italian sociologist born in 1848, had something to say about this. Paredo believed that "leaders maintain themselves in power by. . .bringing into the governing class. . .individuals who might prove dangerous to the governing group. If such recruiting does not take place, in the absence of a free use of force, sooner or later there will be an uprising. . ." (4, p. 567).

All of this is to say that if black and brown people, poor people, and young people were invited to help make the rules of the game, maybe they would be more inclined to abide by these rules. I would warn, however, that their participation will tend to change the rules and the way in which the rules are enforced. Also, new participants will tend to evolve new games. This is as it should be in a democracy. As it is, the rules that currently govern our communities and their institutions are made by decision-making structures whose members are predominantly white, affluent, and adult. These are today's dominant people of power. Bertrand Russell has called the "love of power one of the strongest of human motives" (6, p. 10). A cardinal principle about power is this: People who have it are reluctant to share it. The dominant people of power must learn how to share their power with subdominants. Otherwise, there is no alternative but to force the social change required by revolutionary action that could evolve if subdominants are not involved in the decision-making structures.

References

1. Allen, James E. 1967. "Testimony of Dr. James E. Allen, Jr., Commissioner of Education, State of New York." *Hearing before the United States Commission on Civil Rights in Rochester, New York, 16-17 September 1966.* Washington, D.C.: U.S. Government Printing Office.
2. Brookover, Wilbur B. 1955. *A Sociology of Education.* New York: American Book Company.
3. Clinard, Marshall. 1966. *Slums and Community Development.* New York: The Free Press.
4. Crawford, Rex. 1948. "Representative Italian Contributions to Sociology: Paredo, Louis, Vaccaro, Gino, and Sighele." In *Introduction to the History of Sociology.* Edited by Harry Elmer Barnes. Chicago: University of Chicago Press.
5. Moynihan, Daniel Patrick. 1969. *Maximum Feasible Misunderstanding.* New York: The Free Press.
6. Russell, Bertrand. 1962. *Power.* New York: Barnes and Noble.
7. Willie, Charles V. 1968. "New Perspectives in School-Community Relations." *Journal of Negro Education* 37 (Summer 1968).

10

A Historical Framework
for Multicultural Education

Meyer Weinberg

A black psychiatrist recently wrote:

> We said we'd like the National Institute of Mental Health to
> set up an institute or task force to study racism or white
> supremacy. They didn't say they wouldn't set up such a task
> force or institute. They said we will set up an institute to
> study minority groups. In other words, "we won't study ourselves,
> but we will study you."[1]

A comprehensive study of racism, which must form a central part
of multicultural education, needs to be viewed as a reciprocal
exploration of majority and minority.

The American public school long ago was forced into the service
of prevailing racial conceptions. For decades, in both the North and
the South, outright exclusion of minority children and denigration
of their cultures were standard practices. Today, whether by design
or thoughtlessness, many of the practices still abound. A historical
study can reveal some of their roots and thereby provide educators
with a more realistic understanding of the dimensions of the problem.

One large group of minorities was incorporated within U.S.
society by force and violence—including enslavement and conquest.

Copyright © 1974 by Meyer Weinberg

These minorities include blacks, Mexican Americans, American Indians (Native Americans), and Puerto Ricans. Today, their children make up about a fifth of all public-school children in the United States. The educational fate of their children has been and continues to be determined largely by the relative sociopolitical power their parents exercise. Over the long sweep of American history, the four minorities constitute prime sources of valuable land and low-cost labor. The dominant white community succeeded in gaining advantageous access to these resources through its control of government and armed power. Denied an adequate basis of self-support, the minority people were compelled to occupy a position of extreme economic dependence. Because of the localistic organization of public education in this country, the combination of dependence and powerlessness of the four minorities was translated into inadequate schooling, or the absence of it, wherever these minorities were found.

Let us review in a summary way the educational experiences of the four minorities. Special emphasis is placed on black Americans; space limitations preclude further detailed treatment.

Black Americans

From Slavery to 1865

By 1860 more than 1.3 million slaves were children under ten years of age, while another 1.1 million were between ten and nineteen years old. Virtually none attended school. Under the rule of compulsory ignorance, it ws illegal in most Southern states to teach slaves to read or write. Frederick Douglass, black abolitionist, testified from personal experience that the prohibitory laws were obeyed almost universally. A handful of slaves became literate, however, because a knowledge of letters was necessary at work, because of personal relations with the master's children, or by attendance at secret schools. Even when a slave was literate, the law forbade instruction of his or her own children.

Over a quarter million free blacks in the South fared only slightly better. Some attended public schools; in 1850 an average of about 250 black children were enrolled in each of the sixteen slave states. Even this tiny number shrank during the 1850s. A number attended secret schools that were located in many Southern towns. A few private institutions were begun by blacks, but these foundered on the rocks of poverty and official hostility. Some free blacks learned their letters in sabbath schools. Even modest success alarmed slaveholders and other whites and so after a time instruction in reading was dropped. In 1840, a total of fifteen black sabbath schools in the South enrolled fewer than 1,500 students. All were taught by memory rather than mastery of the written word. Apprenticeship opened literacy to some, because masters were obliged by law to instruct apprentices. During the first quarter of the nineteenth century, however, such stipulations were removed from the law in a number of states.

Free Blacks in the North to 1865

Nearly 250,000 blacks in the North lived in urban centers, for the most part. Unlike their Southern cousins, they were free to move from one place to another and were able to communicate to a much greater degree. Their children were far more likely to find the door of the public school open than was the case down South. Yet, in the main, black children were excluded from the burgeoning public-school system. Often, black parents paid school taxes only to find their children forbidden to attend the schools. Nothing if not realistic, black parents demanded separate schools where black children could not gain entrance to the "common" school. Even within a single Northern state, policies differed. Segregation was the dominant rule in Boston until 1855, but in New Bedford the schools were truly open to all.

In Ohio, although blacks did not have the right to vote, they nevertheless conducted a successful campaign in the state legislature to force public financing of separate schools. In 1853, before the change in policy, only one-tenth of school-age black youth attended public schools; by 1862 the proportion more than quintupled. In other states, such as Pennsylvania and Illinois, legislators were adamant and resisted black efforts.

Once public schools were attained for blacks, parents advanced to an attack upon the principle of separation. When the blacks of Nantucket were reminded in 1842 that they had *their own school*, they replied in a public protest meeting, "We are weary of this kind of honor or distinction."[2] Organized school boycotts by black parents pried open the schools of numerous Northern communities. These included Boston, Nantucket, and Salem, Massachusetts, as well as Rochester, Buffalo, and Lockport, New York.

Wherever they were schooled, and whether or not they received any schooling, black children faced certain special problems. One was the pervasive racism that expressed itself in the form of sweeping employment discrimination. "You can hardly imagine," declared John Rock, the first black lawyer to argue before the U.S. Supreme Court, "the humiliation and contempt a colored lad must feel in graduating the first in a class, and then being rejected everywhere else because of his color."[3] Another problem was the doctrine of racial superiority that called forth feelings of self-depreciation among black children. In 1865, for example, a black newspaper in New Orleans reported that segregated schools operated to "perpetuate from childhood the infatuation of the white, and [to] prompt the black to retaliate by enmity or envy. . . ."[4]

Black Education 1865-1950

In the South, the end of the Civil War brought a new era in black education. The movement for education, wrote W. E. B. DuBois, "started with the Negroes themselves and they continued to form the dynamic force behind it."[5] Blacks contributed money, labor, and building materials—and countless children for whom they finally saw a realistic possibility of educating. Supplementary help came from Northern, white missionary ogranizations—who contributed teachers, money, and school supplies—and the federal Freedman's Bureau, which for several years provided some school buildings and maintenance expenses.

By 1870, one-tenth of all black school-age children were enrolled in school, a very large increase over the 1860 figure of two percent. Only when black children could gain entrance to public schools in the South would the figure rise significantly. Black entry depended crucially upon the attainment of political power. From the late 1860s to the late 1870s, blacks voted and were elected to public office throughout the South. One of the very first fruits of these democratic labors was statutory provision for educating black children at public expense. By 1880 one-third of all school-age black children in the country attended public schools. This meant more than a threefold increase had occurred during the 1870s.

With changing political fortunes, however, the direction of black public education changed abruptly. During the quarter century following 1880, blacks in the South were deprived of the right to vote; the last black member of the U.S. Congress until the present day left office in 1901; lynching became an extralegal means of terrorizing black citizens; the U.S. Supreme Court ruled in 1896 that racial segregation was constitutional (*Plessy vs. Ferguson*) and three years later that a state might close down a black school in order to conserve funds for use at a white school, thus disabling effectively the educational significance of the 14th Amendment (the Cumming case).

School authorities throughout the South regularly diverted state school aid from its designated use at black schools. This was accomplished by the state legislature appropriating equal per-pupil funds that county school boards then spent primarily on white children. By the 1920s and 1930s, Southern counties spent five to twenty times more on white than on black children.

The color line was strictly enforced for both students and teachers. After Reconstruction, segregation of teachers became the rule, especially in rural areas. Black teachers were trained in institutions of meager quality. Southern states consistently refused to appropriate sufficient funds to raise the quality of such training. Black teachers were paid exceedingly low salaries, even by Southern standards. After the 1880s their standards of employment sank, even as the enrollment of black children expanded. Consequently, they lacked realistic incentives to seek further training. In Mississippi, for example, while white teachers could attend tuition-free teachers' colleges part time during the entire school year, black teachers had available only a six-week summer school, which was supported for the most part by their tuition.

Black teachers were expected to respect the system of segregation and discrimination. One black teacher who was employed to teach in a black school in Birmingham, Alabama, during the mid-1920s was told by a school-board interviewer:

> Remember, you did not create the race problem and neither did I. But it is here, and it is here to stay. I want you to go back to Slater School and teach those little Negro boys and girls how to stay in their places and grow up to be good useful citizens.[6]

It was not unusual for school officials to select a worse-prepared applicant if he or she "would maintain the point of view of the whites."[7] Often, influential whites would repay faithful black personal servants by gaining their appointment as teachers in black schools even though they lacked any formal qualifications whatsoever.

During the thirty years following 1880, black Americans tended to remain in the South. By 1910, only eleven percent of all blacks lived outside the South. The ones who did, however, were concentrated in cities and their children had unusual access to the public schools, at least in contrast to the situation in the South. Yet, racially discriminatory schooling for black children remained the rule throughout the North.

In Illinois, at the end of the Civil War, black children were not counted in the apportionment of state aid nor did blacks receive refunds of the school taxes they paid, as the law required. The legislature finally omitted the word *white* from the school law in 1872, and two years later penalties were provided for attempting to exclude black children from the public schools. In southern Illinois especially, the law meant little. By the opening of the present century, racially segregated schools were almost universal in that part of the state. Neither the courts nor state school officials interfered with many of these illegal practices.

In larger metropolitan centers, such as Chicago, numerous schools had become predominantly black by the close of the 1920s. Devices utilized by school authorities to encourage segregation included the building of branch schools nearby the main building in order to direct black children away from the latter. Black teachers were segregated as well. At times, they were excluded altogether from Chicago Normal College, graduation from which was a prerequisite for teaching in the city schools. At other times, a quota on black enrollees seemed to be in effect. Black applicants for teaching positions were generally assigned to predominantly black schools. This extended also to the assignment of substitute teachers. School resources were allocated in discriminatory ways. During the 1930s, for example, numerous black children were crowded into schools that operated on a double shift, consequently with an abbreviated school day. The same pattern persisted into the 1960s despite repeated avowals by authorities that the practice had ended.

After World War II, racially based inequalities existed throughout the state of Illinois. In Edwardsville, for example, two racially separate high schools existed. The white one had a four-year curriculum—while the black one ran only three years. State authorities refused to take remedial action even though the State Superintendent of Public Instruction listed white and black schools separately in the official state school directory.

New York City

By 1920, New York City contained the largest black population of any U.S. city. The number rose from 28,000 in 1880 to 169,000 in 1920; by 1940, more than a half million blacks lived there. Before World War I black children made up less than five percent of the total enrollment. They performed as well as or somewhat below the level achieved by white students. During the 1920s, many students who were newcomers from the South, and had attended short-term rural black schools there, needed special help. A principal in one New York City school provided smaller classes for newcomers. In another school the curriculum was watered down and there were introduced such Southernlike subjects as "millinery, dressmaking, practical homemaking, industrial art, and cooking."[8]

Some of the discrimination in New York City was moderated by the presence of greater organization in the black community. The NAACP had its national headquarters in that city and staff members frequently concerned themselves with school affairs. During the early 1920s, for example, the use of double-shift classes was not closely related to the presence of black children. As mentioned earlier, in Chicago the situation was less favorable.

During the Depression of the 1930s, school problems became communitywide issues in Harlem. Complaints were heard of severe overcrowding, inadequate curriculum, discriminatory reading materials, deliberate segregation, and underrepresentation of blacks in teaching and school governance. Municipal authorities, despite their reputation for liberal politics, failed to acknowledge the seriousness of the complaints and ignored them. In 1935, Mayor Fiorella La Guardia suppressed a critical report on Harlem's schools that he had commissioned. More than forty years later, the report had still not been published.

Various groups rallied black parents to bring pressure upon the school board. The Junior Council of the NAACP worked toward this end in Brooklyn. It found in a survey that some 6,000 school-age black children out of a total of 16,000 were not in school. Teachers were accused of a lack of understanding of black students. The Committee for Better Schools in Harlem, formed in 1936, served as a means whereby many black parents learned to formulate specific demands of the school system. Large-scale delegations conferred often with school officials.

Discrimination against black students existed in the high schools. Three high schools enrolling large numbers of Harlem youth had neither opportunities for academic nor commercial curricula. In 1940, a vocational guidance counselor in a Harlem junior-high school charged that specialized-trades high schools were rejecting black students on the ground that "if we cannot place the boy in the job for which we are to train him, then it is futile to give him the training. . . ."[9] Black-community spokesmen objected and met with counselors in Harlem schools, but no change in school policy resulted.

Residential Segregation

Beginning with World War I, very large-scale black migration northward began. As the newcomers entered the cities, they found residential areas increasingly segregated by race. From 1910 to 1916, Southern and border cities legislated to bar blacks from certain neighborhoods. After these enactments were ruled unconstitutional in 1917, other means were used, in both the North and the South, to reach the same ends. Real-estate organizations undertook to regulate black-residential expansion so as to maintain and expand a solid area of black housing. Members of such groups were forbidden to sell or rent property to a black if he would be the first to enter a presently all-white block.

Northern schools incorporated these same racial patterns into their organization. Attendance areas were redrawn to separate black from white children. In rapidly changing areas school boards often created optional attendance areas with the most recent racial statistics. The grade span of predominantly black schools was sometimes extended so as to prevent children in these schools from going on to a nearby advanced white school. At times, black students were placed in a separate room, even in the basements. Schools designed for black students were located in the growing number of solidly black residential areas. In order to minimize protest at these measures from arising within the school systems, blacks were not appointed to school boards and higher managerial posts.

Between 1865 and 1950, blacks in America succeeded in creating an education tradition in the face of extraordinary opposition. Events of these years documented lavishly DuBois's dictum that "probably never in the world have so many oppressed people tried in every possible way to educate themselves."[10]

The mid-twentieth century marked a turning point in the history of black America. Black leadership took hold of the movement for equality, unprecedented numbers of blacks joined in, and the movement became national in scope. Fundamental to the developments was a persistent black initiative that was ubiquitous and increasingly effective. In time, these events forced a reformulation of national public policies.

Southern Schools 1950-1965

By 1950 black teachers in the South had succeeded in challenging the historic racial differentials in education by court victories on behalf of salary equalization. From 1937 to 1951, the average black teacher's salary increased from 52.5 percent of a white's salary to 87.2 percent. During the same period, black parents filed and won numerous lawsuits demanding equalization of school facilities and programs. Southern state governments tried to deflect the movement by a rapid but highly spotty program of improvement of black-school facilities. The actual change was minimal. During the years 1934-51, for example, the dollar gap in per-pupil expenditures between black and white fell only from $53.85 to $50.15.

The failure of equalization led the black movement to challenge head-on the principle of segregation. In 1954, the U.S. Supreme Court ruled in *Brown vs. Board of Education of Topeka* that "separate educational facilities are inherently unequal," and thus laid to rest the ancient doctrine that separate schools were constitutionally permissible so long as the facilities were equal. Unfortunately, the tribunal failed to establish a timetable for desegregation. Consequently, all but a small fraction of segregation continued in force. Efforts of black parents to press school boards to implement *Brown* foundered. Such petitioners often lost their jobs as a result; if sharecroppers, they were frequently evicted; credit was cut off. Legal evasions by states of the obligation to desegregate, on the other hand, were highly successful. In the absence of executive concern and in the face of continued refusal by the federal judiciary to enforce *Brown*, little was done. Nearly a decade after that ruling, in 1963-64, only 1.2 percent of the South's 2.9 million black schoolchildren attended desegregated schools. More attended such schools in the border states.

The full price of Southern segregation did not become evident in detail until academic achievement data were released in the 1950s and 1960s. Everywhere in the South, black children—schooled for generations in presumably equal-if-separate institutions—were found to lag years behind the achievement of white children. When border cities desegregated schools, tracking systems were frequently introduced to perpetuate the segregation under a common roof. Black children most frequently were assigned to the lowest tracks and typically remained there for the duration of their schooling. As a consequence, both the separation and the deprivation persisted.

An enduring basis for educational change was laid in the years 1950-65 when a black-led civil-rights movement arose in the South. In campaigns staffed by numerous students, thousands of adult blacks were encouraged to register to vote. The persistence of Southern civil-rights workers elevated the demands for equality onto national levels of political concern. The North also joined the civil-rights movement.

Northern Schools 1950-65

As of mid-century, black children in the North attended essentially segregated schools, which were systematically inferior to white schools in the same communities. An achievement gap of black children behind white children was the rule, whether in Berkeley, California, New York City, Chicago, or Bridgeport, Connecticut.

In New York City, black psychologist Kenneth B. Clark led an interracial movement that condemned Northern segregation to be as pernicious as the Southern type. He charged in 1954 that inferior education in the elementary schools ensured that black children "cannot compete with other children in high school."[11] Black and white leaders organized protests aimed at eliminating deliberate and other segregation in the city's schools. Some small steps brought only minimal change. The school board resisted any further steps. In Chicago, the black community protested the discriminatory distribution of school resources and low academic achievement. Large-scale school boycotts followed. In other cities, similar complaints were voiced and little palpable change ensued.

The burgeoning civil-rights movement, North and South, led in 1963-64 to the passage of the Civil Rights Act of 1964. It placed in the hands of the executive branch of the federal government a tool of great potential in effecting change in the schools. This was Title VI of the law, which forbade the racially discriminatory use of federal funds by schools or other recipients of federal grants. Noncompliance was to be followed by a cutoff of funds.

"This legislation," wrote Dr. Martin Luther King, Jr., "was first written in the streets."[12] Action in the streets was still required after passage of the law. During 1965-69 black children and adults participated in an extraordinarily large number of demonstrative actions on behalf of desegregation. In the South, blacks were almost always the organizing and sole participating parties. In the North, they led actions that were frequently interracial.

Black demonstrative action built a solid bedrock beneath the shifts of public policy. During the last years of the Johnson administration, devotion to civil-rights enforcement lagged seriously. The new Nixon administration slowed enforcement even more. Federal courts, including the U.S. Supreme Court, quickly adopted an activist stance and took up the slack. Between 1968 and 1973, several significant rulings extended the *Brown* doctrine far beyond the confines of the 1954 case.

In 1968, the Supreme Court ruled in *Green* that the time for "deliberate speed" had run out and that "the burden on a school board today is to come forward with a [desegregation] plan that promises realistically to work, and promises realistically to work now." In 1969, in the *Alexander* case, the high court directed the state of Mississippi to desegregate immediately. In October 1969, at the time of the decision, nearly nine out of ten black children in the state attended all-black schools. Within three months, the proportion plummeted to one out of ten. In 1971, in the *Swann* case, the court, taking judicial cognizance of residential segregation, held that desegregation plans need not be limited to neighborhood or "walk-in" schools. It was permissible to assign children to a school to which they needed to be bused or otherwise transported. In 1973, the court decided *Keyes*, involving the Denver, Colorado school system. Though the ruling was stated in severely limited terms, it all but eliminated the traditional defense of Northern school boards that school segregation was simply a neutral response to housing segregation. Once a court found that an element of significant conscious intent to segregate had been present, a presumption of sweeping intent could be inferred. This reduced the burden of proof that had hitherto been the responsibility of plaintiffs in desegregation lawsuits.

Approaching the last quarter of the twentieth century, black Americans were succeeding in placing before public schools the challenge of equal opportunity. Supported increasingly by judicial authority, they demanded revision of traditional structures that were buttressed by racially exclusionary practices. From the perspective of more than a century, black children had more practical opportunity to learn than ever before. Most of these improvements, however, resulted from the initiative of organized blacks. Few, if any, had originated with the schools or the learned professions.

Other Minorities

Mexican Americans, American Indians, and Puerto Ricans shared one central characteristic with blacks—all were incorporated originally within American society by force. Historically, Mexican Americans comprised a low-wage labor supply in the Southwest. Accorded the bottom rung on the social ladder in that area, their children were denied equal educational rights. During the first third of the twentieth century, a number of Texas counties failed to provide any public schools for them. In more cases, extralegally segregated schools were made available. These institutions were startlingly inferior in every major respect. In many Texas communities the black schools were in better shape than the counterparts of the

Mexican Americans. Schools consistently attempted to denigrate the Mexican-American culture, outlawing the use of Spanish not only in the classroom but even in the schoolyard. Opportunities for secondary schooling were all but absent for Mexican Americans before the 1930s. Not until the 1960s, as a consequence of widespread protest movements among Mexican Americans, did the schools begin to reexamine their practices with respect to this group.

There was no unified American Indian approach to schooling. Native American responses varied from that of the Cherokees, who in the nineteenth century created an autonomous school system, to that of numerous other American Indian people, who rejected outright any adaptation to white schooling. No Indian tribe, however, was monolithic in its attitude toward white-sponsored schools. Almost everywhere opposing viewpoints on the issue were in evidence. Among the Hopi, for example, the split was profound and enduring.

White society coveted the land occupied by Indians and frequently sought to utilize Indian labor for low wages. Rejected by white society was any thought of adapting to or even countenancing Native American culture. White ways were regarded as civilized, while Indian ways were characterized as savagery. Dominant white society—including government, missionaries, and local business interests near the reservations—viewed education as the avenue for destruction of American Indian culture. Virtually absent from white discussion was any recognition that a mutually respectful adaptation could be worked out. Only by the late 1960s did the possibility enter the realm of public discussion.

Puerto Ricans did not constitute a major presence in American schools until after World War II. During the 1940s and 1950s, the average annual net migration from Puerto Rico to the mainland rose sharply to 18,794 and then to 41,212. Between 1945 and 1962, the number of Puerto Rican migrants constituted 85 percent of all Puerto Rican migration since 1900.

Puerto Rican children and their teachers were almost complete strangers. In the early postwar years, about three-quarters of the migrant children did not speak English, but far more of their teachers could not speak Spanish. Language barriers were defined by the school system as learning barriers. Since by 1965 Puerto Rican children made up one-fifth of all public-school students in New York City, the scale of academic failure was sweeping. Preliminary steps to change traditional practices that seemed to ensure failure began to be taken during the 1960s. Basic to these new currents was the formation of a new cultural and community self-consciousness among Puerto Ricans on the mainland.

As we have seen, the children of the four minorities thus far discussed shared certain common experiences in the public schools. It would, however, be a major distortion to equate their experiences with the ones of other minorities. The fate of each minority was determined in large part by the circumstances existing at the time that minority entered U.S. history. During the late nineteenth century, the American economy more easily absorbed illiterate workers than seventy-five years later.

The pre-Civil War immigrant typically came from Northern and Western Europe. While the nascent public-school systems kept the poorest Irish immigrants at a distance, most other immigrant children entered the schools with little resistance. After the Civil War, there was no "typical immigrant" response to public schooling. When Russian Jews streamed to the United States between 1880 and 1920, they viewed American schools from the perspective of having been officially excluded from many Russian schools. They also arrived at a time when American industry was developing numerous white-collar jobs and thereby a labor market for high-school and college-educated workers. In addition, by and large, Jewish students were welcomed in the schools.

German Catholics who came to Wisconsin and the Midwest in large numbers between 1850 and 1890 established parochial schools that were conducted in the German language. When the state legislature outlawed the use of any language in school other than English, the Germans organized a political campaign and the law was repealed. Poles in Buffalo, New York, also conducted parochial schools in the Polish language in a largely successful effort to conserve their cultural heritage.

European immigrants were better able to provide their children with a public-school education because of advantages they held over blacks, Mexican Americans, American Indians, and Puerto Ricans. The former came to occupy higher economic positions, most of them unconnected with the degree of education attained. They possessed full political rights in their communities and exercised them, although to varying degrees. And their right to attend public schools was never challenged in court. The latter, however, were consigned to the lowest levels of the American economy, including forced labor. Political means to remedy community problems were denied them for many years. They were subjected to legal segregation, both by statute and school board action. Asian Americans, especially the Chinese, were somewhere in between both groups. While they were, for the most part, voluntary immigrants, they suffered from legally segregated schools in California and from extraordinary discriminations in community life.

One or Two Melting Pots?

Once we were asked to believe that American life shaped a single, homogeneous breed of people, each equal to the other and all sharing a common culture. It is no improvement, however, to be told now that there are, after all, *two* melting pots—one for the dominant, Anglo whites and the other for all the minorities in American society.

The new myth of two melting pots imagines that all minorities share a common fate. They are "ethnics." Anglo whites, presumably, are nonethnics. The old myth erected Anglo culture as the measure of all others. The new one performs the same task by staking out mere footnotes and appendixes for each separate minority, while reserving the page proper for the "main" story. Such a portrayal is said to document the cultural pluralism of America. Somehow, the plurality of pots is to result in their equality.

A strong point of the older concept of one melting pot was its stress on the factual integration of immigrant and native in the general economy and, to a lesser extent, in politics. It erred, however, in believing that the absorption of minorities expanded their rights or even their dignity. Just how the minorities were absorbed—or not absorbed—has been in large part a product of history. There would seem to be no warrant in American history for single *or* plural melting pots.

Rather than draining the individuality of each minority group in an effort to create a faceless and anonymous mass, it would seem more serviceable to distinguish among minority groups and view each as embodying a distinctive set of experiences and traditions. Clearly, the experience of minority groups is differentially salient for national development. Black history is central to many basic issues in American history. The importance of Slavic workers in building American basic industries was very great, if unheralded. Scandinavian groups have had a more regional and less of a national impact. And so on. Not to be overlooked are the groups that remained less than a majority but avoided the label of minority. The English immigrants, for instance, apparently lost all signs of being an ethnic group.

Racism, Culture, and Society

Few immigrant groups escaped altogether the hurt of discrimination and prejudice. Religious and nationality factors provided grounds for deprivation of immigrant groups. But a special fury has been reserved for blacks, Mexican Americans, American Indians, and Puerto Ricans. This is the fury of racism, a doctrine of racial or ethnic superiority, including advocacy of differential rewards based on presumed differences. By incorporating the allocation of differential rewards into institutions such as the economy, education, and government, dominant white society created an impersonal system that served racist purposes very effectively.

Cultural denigration of certain minorities by the dominant society formed part of the racial system. While, however, minority cultures were regarded as part of the inferior group to be scorned, these were lesser targets. In U.S. history, conquest of minorities was motivated by material gain rather than by ideological hatred of unfamiliar cultures.

Reversal of racist trends would seem to rest upon the possibility of changing the position of these minorities in American society as a whole. This, the schools cannot possibly achieve by themselves. To be sure, they have hardly begun to try. The proper sphere of the schools would seem to be in the cultural area, all the time realizing that the cultural aspect of minority status is not the most fundamental.

Multicultural Education

Race has been part of the curriculum ever since we have had public schools.[13] Before the Civil War, American schools accepted and perpetuated racial values. Textbooks treated blacks and other minorities as undesirables. Blacks were often excluded from public schools—North and South—and, when admitted, frequently were forced to sit in a separate part of the classroom.

After the destruction of slavery, exclusion and/or denigration of minority values continued. Except for a moment of enlightenment during Reconstruction, the years 1870-1920 were a low point in the history of race relations in the United States.

During the past half century, interracial attendance has become a reality in many schools. Today, one-seventh of all children attend an interracial or interethnic public school. Yet the heritage of the past still weighs heavily upon the American classroom. Practices originally created to serve racist purposes linger on as thoughtless monuments to the past. Textbooks remain largely untouched by newer currents of thought. The curriculum is still inadequately responsive to recent research, especially in the social sciences. But the greatest impediment to essential change is the ethnic isolation that still characterizes the American classroom.

Over the past fifty years, interracial education has taken several forms. The human relations approach evolved during the 1920s and held the field, so to speak, for a generation. The method essentially was based on the concept of tolerance. It was a defensive teaching strategy, aimed principally at counterbalancing an overbearing majority sentiment that rejected equally differences of color, language, and national custom. Much attention was paid to explaining cultural peculiarities.

Interpersonal conflict was seen as a clash of single individuals. Prejudice was regarded as a failing of individuals who lacked an ability to see others as individuals. It was hoped that this lack could be remedied by the acquisition of information about the minority object, too weak to prevail against the majority; thus, the human relations approach was inevitably moralistic in its appeal.

A second approach may be called *interracial*. This method frankly acknowledged the fact of antiblack prejudice and distinguished it from the area of simple culture conflict. The unique role of the black in American life was seen as a central distinguishing characteristic of American society. Concern with individual prejudice extended now to exploration of discrimination. Disability and deprivation were found to be aspects of group existence in the United States. Blacks were seen as a subculture with their own distinctive development. Great efforts were expended on discovering the manifold forms of group discrimination against blacks and American Indians especially. Discrimination against blacks was found to be far more resistant than that based on religion, language, or national origin.

In the classroom, spreading celebration of events such as Black History Week illustrated the fact of separate existence. It also signaled an affirmation of black accomplishment and initiative. To be sure, it was in the segregated black classroom that the celebration was most likely to adopt such a tone. Only in occasional large, urban schools, integrated in some sense, were similar events celebrated.

The interracial approach was more realistic than the human

relations approach, though it was also defensive in orientation. Children were taught the disability of color in American life. But they failed to learn to conceive of a world without this disability. So far-fetched did such a world seem that the possibility was not discussed.

Today, a third approach—the human rights approach—is in the making. This method presents group differences affirmatively, and its ideology is an unshrinking proclamation of universal equality. Essentially, it is a belief that members of ethnic groups have the absolute right to define their own ethnic status: They will be what they decide. It is neither separatism nor desegregation, but pluralism with equality. The goal is not to be like or with others on principle.

Assimilation is rejected because it assumes lack of worth on the part of the minority. Increasingly, however, the group is viewed in terms of its dignity. (*Dignus* is Latin for *worth*.) Integration as such is rejected as too prescriptive for everyone; instead it becomes one other option that some minority people can select—if they wish. In fact, of course, the option to integrate has almost always remained a white prerogative. Pluralism without equality, as Kenneth B. Clark has noted, is hardly more than a caste system, where each subculture has the right to exist so long as it keeps its "place."

The new movement for human rights thus strains at the seams of the traditional racial order. Even national boundaries are overtaken. If the object now is to win those rights that are common to all mankind, then a worldwide bond emerges to bind all men together. The movement for human rights is therefore internationalist as well; consequently, one hears of a Third World—a combination of people in the former European colonies along with black Americans, Mexican Americans, American Indians, and Asian Americans.

None of the approaches discussed above is unconnected with the others. One may stress cultural distinctiveness in any of them. It will, however, take much hard thought by educators to formulate an effective response to the challenge of human rights. Some may be put off by the very newness of the subject. Alas! We cannot wait until this subject "settles down." It is up to us to create the instructional strategies and materials.

Notes

1. Frances Welsing, Washington *Post*, 9 September 1973.
2. *Liberator*, 18 March 1842.
3. *Liberator*, 15 August 1862.

4. New Orleans *Tribune*, February 1965, in *The Negro's Civil War. How American Negroes Felt and Acted During the War for the Union.* edited by James M. McPherson (New York: Vintage, 1967), p. 17.

5. W. E. B. DuBois, "Reconstruction and Its Benefits," *American Historical Review* (1909-1910), p. 782.

6. Ellen Tarry, *The Third Door. The Autobiography of an American Woman* (New York: Guild Press, 1966), p. 79.

7. Carter G. Woodson, *The Rural Negro* (Washington, D.C.: Association for the Study of Negro Life and History, 1930), p. 189.

8. *New York Age*, 10 January 1920.

9. Quoted in Celia Lewis Zitron, *The New York City Teachers Union 1916-1964* (New York: Humanities Press, 1968), p. 90.

10. W. E. B. DuBois, "The United States and the Negro," *Freedomways* (1961), p. 16.

11. Kenneth B. Clark, quoted by Bert E. Swanson in *The Struggle for Equality. School Integration Controversy in New York City* (New York: Hobbs, Dorman, 1966), p. 13.

12. Martin Luther King, Jr. " 'Let Justice Roll Down,' " *Nation*, 15 March 1965, pp. 271-72.

13. This section is taken from Meyer Weinberg, "Introduction: Race and Educational Opportunity," in *Models for Integrated Education*, edited by Daniel U. Levine (Worthington, Ohio: Jones, 1971), pp. 1-3.

11

The "Liberation" of Gary, Indiana

Edward Greer

In silhouette, the skyline of Gary, Indiana, could serve as the perfect emblem of America's industrial might—or its industrial pollution. In the half century since they were built, the great mills of the United States Steel Corporation—once the largest steel complex on earth—have produced more than one-quarter trillion tons of steel. They have also produced one of the highest air-pollution rates on earth. Day and night the tall stacks belch out a ruddy smoke that newcomers to the city find almost intolerable.

Apart from its appalling physical presence, the most striking thing about Gary is the very narrow compass in which the people of the city lead their lives. Three-quarters of the total work force is directly employed by the United States Steel Corporation. About seventy-five percent of all male employment is in durable-goods manufacture and in the wholesale-retail trades, and a majority of this labor force is blue collar. This means that the cultural tone of the city is solidly working class.

But not poor. Most Gary workers own their own homes, and the city's median income is ten percent above the national average [1971]. The lives of these people, however, are parochial, circumscribed, on a tight focus. With the exception of the ethnic clubs, the union, and the Catholic church, the outstanding social edifices in Gary are its bars, gambling joints, and whorehouses.

177

Company Town

The city of Gary was the largest of all company towns in America. The United States Steel Corporation began construction in 1905, after assembling the necessary parcel of land on the Lake Michigan shore front. Within two years, over $40 million had been invested in the project; by now the figure must be well into the billions.

Gary was built practically from scratch. Swamps had to be drained and dunes leveled; a belt-line railroad to Chicago had to be constructed, as well as a port for ore ships and, of course, a vast complex of manufacturing facilities including coke ovens, blast furnaces, and an independent electrical power plant. The city was laid out by corporation architects and engineers and largely developed by the corporation-owned Gary Land Company, which did not sell off most of its holdings until the thirties. Even though the original city plan included locations for a variety of civic, cultural, and commercial uses (though woefully little for park land), an eminent critic, John W. Reps, points out that it "failed sadly in its attempt to produce a community pattern noticeably different or better than elsewhere."

The corporation planned more than the physical nature of the city. It also had agents advertise in Europe and the South to bring in workers from as many different backgrounds as possible to build the mills and to work in them. Today over fifty ethnic groups are represented in the population.

This imported labor was cheap, and it was hoped that cultural differences and language barriers would curtail the growth of a socialist labor movement. The tough, pioneer character of the city and the fact that many of the immigrant workers' families had not yet joined them in this country combined to create a lawless and vice-ridden atmosphere that the corporation did little to curtail. In much more than its genesis and name, then, Gary is indelibly stamped in the mold of its corporate creators.

Labor and the Left

During the course of World War I, government and vigilante repression broke the back of the Socialist party in small-town America, though it was not very strong to begin with. Simultaneously, however, the Left grew rapidly as a political force among the foreign born in large urban centers. As the war continued, labor peace was kept by a combination of prosperity (full employment and overtime), pressures for production in the "national interest," and Wilsonian and corporate promises of an extension of democracy in the workplace after the war was over. The promises of a change in priorities proved empty, and in 1919 the long-suppressed grievances of the steelworkers broke forth. Especially among the unskilled immigrant workers, demands for an industrial union, a reduction of the workday from twelve to eight hours, and better pay and working conditions sparked a spontaneous movement for an industrywide strike.

For a time it appeared that the workers would win the Great Steel Strike of 1919, but, despite the capable leadership of William Z. Foster, the strike was broken. The native white, skilled labor aristocracy refused to support it, and the corporation imported blacks from the South to scab in the mills. This defeat helped set back the prospect of militant, industrial trade unionism for almost a generation. And meanwhile, racism, a consumer-oriented culture (especially the automobile and relaxed sexual mores) and reforms from above (by the mid-twenties the eight-hour day had been voluntarily granted in the mills) combined to prevent the Left from recovering as a significant social force.

It was in this period between World War I and the Depression that a substantial black population came to Gary. Before the war only a handful of black families lived there, and few of them worked in the mills. During World War I, when immigration from abroad was choked off, blacks were encouraged to move to Gary to make up for the labor shortage caused by expanding production. After the war this policy was continued, most spectacularly during the strike, but rather consistently throughout the twenties. In 1920 blacks made up 9.6 percent of the population; in 1930 they were 17.8 percent—and they were proportionately represented in the steel-industry work force.

When the Congress of Industrial Organizations (C.I.O.) was organized during the Depression, an interracial alliance was absolutely essential to the task. In Gary a disproportionate number of the union organizers were black; the Communist party's slogan of "black and white unite and fight" proved useful as an organizing tactic. Nevertheless, it was only during World War II (and not as the result of the radicals' efforts) that black workers made a substantial structural advance in the economy. Demography, wartime full employment, and labor shortages proved more important to the lot of black workers than their own efforts and those of their allies.

As occurred after World War I, and also after the second, there came a repression to counter the growth of the Left. The communist component of the trade-union movement was wiped out, and in the general atmosphere of the early Cold War black people, too, found themselves on the defensive. At the local level in Gary, the remaining trade-union leaders made their peace with the corporation (as well as the local racketeers and Democratic party politicians), while various campaigns in the forties to racially integrate the schools and parks failed utterly.

Finally, in the early fifties, the inherently limited nature of the trade union when organized as a purely defensive institution of the working class—and one moreover that fully accepts capitalist property and legal norms—stood fully revealed. The Steelworkers Union gave up its right to strike over local grievances, which the Left had made a key part of its organizing policy, in return for binding arbitration, which better suited the needs and tempers of the emerging labor bureaucrats.

Corporate Racism

The corporation thus regained effective full control over the work process. As a result, the corporation could increase the amount of profit realized per worker. It could also intensify the special oppression of the black workers; foremen could now assign them discriminatorily to the worst tasks without real union opposition. This corporate racism had the additional benefit of weakening the workers' solidarity. For its part, the union abolished shop stewards, replacing them with one full-time elected "griever." This of course further attenuated rank-and-file control over the union bureaucracy, aided in depoliticizing the workers, and gave further rein to the union's inclination to mediate worker/employer differences at the point of production, rather than sharpen the lines of struggle in the political economy as a whole.

The corporate and union elites justified this process by substantial wage increases, together with other benefits such as improved pension and welfare plans. For these gains a price was paid. Higher product prices, inflation, and a rising tax burden on the workers all ensued from the union's passive acceptance of corporate priorities.

There were extremely important racial consequences as well. For as the union leadership was drawn further and further into complicity with corporate goals, a large segment of the industrial working class found itself in the apparently contradictory position of opposing the needs of the poorest workers for increased social-welfare services. A large part of the material basis for white working-class racism originates here. Gary steelworkers, struggling to meet their home-mortgage payments, are loath to permit increased assessments for additional municipal services, which they view as mostly benefiting black people.

United States Steel

Needless to say, the corporation helped to develop, promote, and protect the Gary working class's new ways of viewing itself and its world.

In the mill, the corporation systematically gave the black workers the dirtiest jobs (in the coke plants, for example) and bypassed them for promotion—especially for the key skilled jobs and as foremen. Nor has that policy changed. Although about a third of the employees in the Gary Works are black, and many of them have high seniority, and although virtually all the foremen are promoted directly from the ranks without needing any special qualifications, there are almost no black (nor Spanish-speaking) foremen. According to figures submitted by the United States Steel Corporation to the Gary Human Relations Commission, as of 31 March 1968, out of a total of 1,011 first-line supervisors (foremen) only 22 were black.

The corporation not only practices racism directly, it also encourages it indirectly by supporting other discriminatory institutions in Gary. Except for some free professionals and small business, the entire business community is a de facto fief of the corporation. The Gary Chamber of Commerce has never to my knowledge differed from the corporation on any matter of substance, though it was often in its economic self-interest to do so. This has been true even with regard to raising the corporation's property assessment, which would directly benefit local business financially. And in its hiring and sales practices, as well as in its social roles, this group is a leading force for both institutional racism and racist attitudes in the community. For instance, it is well known that the local banks are very reluctant to advance mortgage money in black areas of town, thus assuring the physical decline. White workers then draw the reasonable conclusion that the movement of blacks into their neighborhods will be at the expense of the value of their homes and react accordingly. The local media, completely dependent financially on the local business community, can fairly be described as overtly racist. The story of the voting fraud conspiracy to prevent the election of Mayor Richard Hatcher, a black man, did not get into the local paper until days after it made the front page of the New York *Times*.

The newspaper publisher is very close to the national Catholic hierarchy and the local bishop, who in turn is closely linked to the local banks. The church is rhetorically, moderately liberal at the diocesan level, but among the ethnic parishes the clergy are often overtly racist.

Political Considerations

The power of the city government, as is usually the case in this country, is highly fragmented. Its legal and financial authority is inadequate to carry out the public functions for which it bears responsibility. The power of the mayor is particularly limited. State civil-service laws insulate school, welfare, fire, and police personnel from the control of city hall. Administrative agencies control key functions such as urban renewal, the low-income housing authority, sanitation, the park system, and the board of health. Appointive boards, with long and staggered terms of tenure, hire the administrators of these agencies; and although in the long run a skillful mayor can obtain substantial control over their operations, in the short run (especially if there are sharp policy differences) his power may well be marginal.

Two other structural factors set the context in which local government in Gary—and in America generally—is forced to operate. First, key municipal functions increasingly depend upon federal aid; thus, the priorities of the federal government increasingly shape the alternatives and options open to local officials, and their real independence is attenuated.

Second, the tax resources of local governments—resting for the most part on comparatively static real-estate levies—are able to meet the sharply rising costs of municipal services and operations less and less. These costs reflect the increased social costs of production and welfare, costs the corporations are able to pass on to the general public.

This problem is particularly acute in Gary because of the ability of the corporation to remain grossly underassessed. As a result, there are implacable pressures to resist expansion of municipal services, even if the need for them is critical. In particular, since funds go to maintain existing services, it is virtually impossible for a local government to initiate any substantive innovations unless prior funding is assured. In this context, a sustained response to the urban crisis is prevented not only by a fragmentation of power, but also by a lack of economic resources on a scale necessary to obtain significant results.

For the city of Gary, until the election of Mayor Hatcher, it was academic to talk about such considerations as the limits of local government as an instrument of social change and improvement of the general welfare. Before him, municipal government had been more or less content simply to mediate between the rackets on the one hand and the ethnic groups and business community on the other.

The Democratic party, structured through the Lake County machine, was the mechanism for accomplishing a division of spoils and for maintaining at least a formal legitimacy for a government that provided a minimum return to its citizenry. Left alone by the corporation, which subscribed to an inspired policy of live and let live where municipal politics were concerned, this political coalition governed Gary as it saw fit.

In return for the benevolent neutrality of the corporation toward its junior partner, the governing coalition refrained from attempting to raise the corporation's tax assessments or to otherwise insinuate itself into the absolute sovereignty of the corporation over the Gary Works. Air-pollution activities were subjected only to token inspection and control, and, as far as can be ascertained, the Building Department never sent an inspector into the mill. (These and other assertions about improper or shady activities are based on reports from reliable informants and were usually verified by a second source. I served under Mayor Hatcher as director of the Office of Program Coordination until February 1969.)

In this setting—particularly in the absence of a large middle class interested in "good government" reform—politics was little more than a racket, with the city government as the chief spoils. An informal custom grew up that representatives of different ethnic minorities would each hold the mayor's office for one term. The mayor then, in association with the county officials, allegedly sanctioned the organized crime (mostly gambling, liquor, and prostitution) within the community. In effect, the police force and the prosecutor's office allegedly erected and centralized a protection racket with city officials as its directors and organized crime as its client. Very large sums of money were involved, as indicated by the fact that one recent official was described by Internal Revenue officials as having an estimated annual income while in office of $1.5 million.

Besides the racket of protecting criminal activity, other sources of funds contributed to the large illicit incomes of city officials. There were almost 1,000 patronage jobs to distribute to supporters or to sell to friends. There were proceeds from a myriad of business transactions and contracts carried out under municipal authority. Every aspect of municipal activity was drawn into the cash nexus.

For instance, by local ordinance one had to pass an examination and pay a $150 fee for a contractor's license to do repair or construction work within city limits. The licensing statute was enacted to maintain reasonable standards of performance and thus protect the public. In reality, as late as 1967, passing the exam required few skills, except the ability to come up with $1,200 for the relevant officials, or $1,500 if the applicant was unfortunate enough to have black skin.

Gary municipal affairs also had a racist quality. The black population continued to rise until in the early sixties it composed an absolute majority. Yet the benefits of the system just outlined were restricted to the less scrupulous of the leaders of other ethnic groups, which constituted altogether only forty percent of the population. The spoils came from all; they were distributed only among whites.

And this was true not only for illegal spoils and patronage but also for legitimate municipal services. As one example, after Hatcher became mayor, one of the major complaints of the white citizenry concerned the sharp decline in the frequency of garbage collection. This resulted, not from a drop in efficiency of the General Services division, as was often charged, but from the fact that the garbage routes were finally equalized between white and black areas.

In short, the city government was itself just another aspect of the institutionalized structure of racism in Gary. To assure the acquiescence of Gary's blacks to the system, traditional mechanisms of repression were used: bought black politicians and ward leaders, token jobs, the threat of violence against rebels, and the spreading of a sense of impotence and despair. For instance, it was a Gary tradition for the Democratic machine to contribute $1,500 each week to a black ministers' alliance for them to distribute to needy parishioners—with the tacit understanding that when elections came around they would help deliver the vote.

Hatcher's Campaign

The successful insurgency of Richard Gordon Hatcher destroyed the core of this entire relationship.

Hatcher developed what can best be described as a black united front, inasmuch as it embraced all sectors of the black community by social class, occupation, ideology, and temperament. The basis of this united front was a commonly held view that black people as a racial group were discriminated against by the politically dominant forces. Creating it required that Hatcher bridge existing divisions in the black community, which he did by refusing to be drawn into a disavowal of any sector of the black movement either to his left or right—except for those local black politicians who were lackeys of the Democratic machine. Despite immense public pressure, for example, Hatcher refused to condemn Stokley Carmichael, even though scurrilous right-wing literature was widely circulated calling him a tool of Carmichael and Fidel Castro. Actually, the rumor that hurt Hatcher the most was the false assertion that he was secretly engaged to a white campaign worker—and it was so damaging in the black community that special pains had to be taken to overcome it.

[. . .]

It is worth noting that a substantial portion of Hatcher's financial and technical assistance came from a very small group of white liberals and radicals, who, while they played a role disproportionate to their numbers, suffered significant hostility from their white neighbors for involving themselves openly with Hatcher. Their support, however, made it possible for the campaign to appeal, at least rhetorically, to all the citizens on an interracial basis.

Of course, this support in the white community did not translate into votes. When the count was complete in the general election, only thirteen percent of Gary's overwhelmingly Democratic white voters failed to bolt to the Republicans; and if one omits the Jewish professional and business section of town, that percentage falls to six percent (in blue-collar Glen Park)—a figure more explicable by polling-booth error than goodwill.

Even in the Democratic primary against the incumbent mayor, Hatcher barely won, although he had the support of a large majority of the Spanish-speaking vote and overwhelming support (over ninety percent) of the black vote. His victory was possible, moreover, only because the white vote was split almost down the middle due to the entry of an insurgent and popular "backlash" candidate.

Hatcher's primary victory was particularly impressive given the obstacles he had to face. First, his entire primary campaign was run on less than $50,000, while the machine spent an estimated $500,000 in cash on buying black votes alone. Second, the media was openly hostile to Hatcher. And third, efforts were made to physically intimidate the candidate and his supporters. Death threats were common, and many beatings occurred. Without a doubt, the unprecedented action of the Hatcher organization in forming its own self-defense squads was essential in preventing mass intimidation. It was even necessary on primary day for armed groups to force open polls in black areas that would otherwise have remained inoperative.

These extraordinary methods demonstrated both how tenuous are the democratic rights of black people and what amazing organization and determination are necessary to enforce them when real shifts of power appear to be at stake. When the primary results came in, thousands of black citizens in Gary literally danced in the streets with joy; and everyone believed that the old Gary was gone forever.

Hatcher's Temptations

Immediately after the primary victory, the local alignment of forces was to some degree overshadowed by the rapid interposition of national ones. Until Hatcher won the primary, he was left to sink or swim by himself; after he established his own independent base of power, a new and more complex political process began: his reintegration into the national political system.

The county Democratic machine offered Hatcher a bargain: its support and $100,000 for the general election campaign in return for naming the chief of police, corporation counsel, and controller. Naturally, Hatcher refused to accept a deal that would have made him a puppet of the corrupt elements he was determined to oust from power. Thereupon the county machine (and the subdistrict director of the Steelworkers' Union) declared itself for, and campaigned for, the Republican.

But the question was not left there. To allow the Democratic party to desert a candidate solely because he was black would make a shambles of its appeal to black America. And dominant liberal forces within the Democratic party clearly had other positive interests in seeing Hatcher elected. Most dramatically, the Kennedy wing of the Democratic party moved rapidly to adopt Hatcher, offering him sorely needed political support, financial backing, and technical assistance, without any strings attached. By doing this, it both solidified its already strong support from the black community and made it more reasonable for blacks to continue to place their faith in the Democratic party and in the political system as a whole.

As a necessary response to this development (although it might have happened anyway), the Johnson-Humphrey wing of the Democratic party also offered support. And this meant that the governor of Indiana and the Indiana State Democratic party endorsed Hatcher as well—despite the opposition of the powerful Lake County machine. Thus Hatcher achieved legitimacy within the political system—a legitimacy that he would need when it came to blocking a serious voting-fraud plot to prevent his winning the election.

Despite clear evidence of what was happening, the Justice Department nevertheless refused to intervene against this plot until Hatcher's campaign committee sent telegrams to key federal officials warning them that failure to do so would result in a massive race riot for which the federal officials would be held publicly responsible. Only by this unorthodox maneuver, whose credibility rested on Hatcher's known independent appeal and constituency, was the federal executive branch persuaded to enforce the law. Its intervention, striking 5,000 phony names from the voters rolls, guaranteed a Hatcher victory instead of a Hatcher defeat.

The refusal of the Justice Department to move except under what amounted to blackmail indicated that the Johnson-Humphrey wing of the party was not enthusiastic about Hatcher, whose iconoclastic and often radical behavior did not assure that he would behave appropriately after he was in power. But its decision finally to act, together with the readiness of the Kennedy forces to fully back Hatcher, suggests that there was a national strategy into which the Hatcher insurgency could perhaps be fitted.

My own view of that national strategy is that the federal government and the Democratic party were attempting to accommodate themselves to rising black insurgency, and especially electoral insurgency, so as to contain it within the two-party system. This strategy necessitated sacrificing, at least to a degree, vested parochial interests, such as entrenched and corrupt machines.

Furthermore, black insurgency from below is potentially a force to rationalize obsolete local governments. The long-term crisis of the cities, itself reflecting a contradiction between public gain and private interest, has called forth the best reform efforts of the corporate liberal elite. Centered in the federal government, with its penumbra of foundations, law firms, and universities, the political forces associated with this rationalizing process were most clearly predominant in the Kennedy wing of the Democratic party.

The economic forces whose interests are served by this process are first the banks, insurance companies, and other sections of large capital heavily invested in urban property and, more generally, the interests of corporate capital as a whole—whose continued long-range profit and security rest on a stable, integrated, and loyal population.

Thus the support given to Hatcher was rational to the system as a whole and not at all peculiar, even though it potentially implied economic and political loss for the corporation, United States Steel, whose operations on the spot might become more difficult. The interests of the governing class as a whole and of particular parts of it often diverge; this gap made it possible for Hatcher to achieve some power within the system. How these national factors would shape the amount and forms of power Hatcher actually obtained became quite evident within his first year of office.

Mosaic of Black Power

When I arrived in the city five months after the inauguration, my first task was to aid in the process of bringing a semblance of order out of what can fairly be described as administrative chaos.

When the new administration took over city hall in January 1968 it found itself without the keys to offices, with many vital records missing (for example, the file on the United States Steel Corporation in the controller's office), and with a large part of the city government's movable equipment stolen. The police force, for example, had so scavenged the patrol cars for tires and batteries that about ninety percent of the cars were inoperable. This sort of thing is hardly what one thinks of as a normal process of American government. It seems more appropriate to a bitter ex-colonial power. It is, in fact, exactly what happened as the French left Sekou Toure's Guinea.

There were no funds available. This was because the city council had sharply cut the municipal budget the previous summer in anticipation of a Hatcher victory. It intended, if he lost, to legislate a supplemental appropriation. But when he won without bringing in a council majority with him, its action assured that he would be especially badly crippled in his efforts to run the city government with a modicum of efficiency. Moreover, whenever something went wrong, the media could and did blame the mayor for his lack of concern or ability.

Not only did Richard Hatcher find his position sabotaged by the previous administration even before he arrived, but holdovers, until they were removed from their positions, continued to circumvent his authority by design or accident as well. And this comparatively unfavorable situation extended to every possible sphere of municipal activities.

Another problem was that the new administrators had to take over the management of a large, unwieldly, and obsolete municipal system without the slightest prior executive experience. That there were no black people in Gary with such experience in spite of the high degree of education and intelligence in the black community is explicable only in terms of institutionalized racism—blacks in Gary were never permitted such experiences and occupational roles. Hatcher staffed his key positions with black men who had been schoolteachers, the professional role most closely analogous to running a government bureaucracy. Although several of these men were, in my view, of outstanding ability, they still had to learn everything by trial and error, an arduous and painful way to maintain a complex institution.

Furthermore, this learning process was not made any easier by the unusually heavy demands placed on the time of the mayor and his top aides by the national news media, maneuvering factions of the Democratic party, a multiplicity of civil-rights organizations, universities, voluntary associations, and others who viewed the mayor as a celebrity to be importuned, exploited, or displayed. This outpouring of national interest in a small, parochial city came on top of and was almost equal to, the already heavy work load of the mayor.

Nor were there even clerical personnel to answer the mail and phone calls, let alone rationally respond to the deluge. The municipal budget provided the mayor with a single secretary; it took most of the first summer to make the necessary arrangements to pay for another two secretaries for the mayor's own needs. One result was that as late as June 1968, there was still a two-month backlog of personal mail, which was finally answered by much overtime work.

In addition to these problems there were others, not as common to American politics, such as the threat of violence, which had to be faced as an aspect of daily life. The problem of security was debilitating, especially after the King and Kennedy assassinations. In view of the mayor's aggressive drive against local organized crime, the race hatred whipped up during and after the campaign by the right wing and the history of violence in the steel town, this concern with security was not excessive, and maintaining it was a problem. Since the police were closely linked with the local Right, it was necessary to provide the mayor with private bodyguards. The presence of this armed and foreboding staff impaired efficiency without improving safety, especially since the mayor shrugged off the danger and refused to cooperate with these security efforts.

In addition, the tremendous amounts of aid we were offered by foundations, universities, and federal officials proved to be a mixed blessing. The time needed to oversee existing processes was pre-empted by the complex negotiations surrounding the development and implementation of a panoply of new federal programs. There had never been a Concentrated Employment Program in Gary, nor a Model Cities Program, nor had the poverty program been locally controlled. Some of these programs were not only new to Gary, but they had not been implemented anywhere else either. The municipal bureaucracy, which under previous administrations had deliberately spared itself the embarrassment of federal audits, did not have the slightest idea as to how to utilize or to run these complex federal programs. Moreover, none of the experts who brought this largesse to Gary had a clear understanding of how it was to be integrated into the existing municipal system and social structure. These new federal programs sprang up overnight—new bureaucracies, ossified at birth—and their actual purposes and effects bore little relation to the legislative purposes of the congressional statutes that authorized them.

Needless to say, ordinary municipal employees experienced this outside assistance as a source of confusion and additional demoralization, and their efficiency declined further. Even the new leadership was often overwhelmed by, and defensive before, the sophisticated Eastern federal bureaucrats and private consultants who clearly wanted only to help out one of America's first elected black mayors of a major Northern city. The gifts, in other words, carried a fearful price.

Bureaucratic Enemies

Except for the uniformed officials and the schools, which were largely outside the mayor's control, the standing city bureaucracy was a key dilemma for Mayor Hatcher.

The mayor had run on a reform program. His official campaign platform placed "good government" first, ahead of even tax reform and civil rights. Hatcher was deeply committed to eliminating graft and corruption, improving the efficiency of municipal government—especially the delivery of services to those sectors of the citizenry that had been most deprived—and he did not view his regime as merely the substitution of black faces for white ones in positions of power.

But he also had a particular historic injustice to rectify: the gross underrepresentation of blacks in the city government, and their complete exclusion from policymaking positions. Moreover, implicit in his campaign was a promise to reward his followers, who were mostly black. (At least most participants in the campaign assumed such a promise; Hatcher himself never spoke about the matter.)

Consequently, there was tremendous pressure from below to kick out everyone not covered by civil-service protection and substitute all-black personnel in their places. But to do so would have deepened the hostility of the white population and probably weakened Hatcher's potential leverage in the national Democratic party. He resisted this pressure, asserting that he believed in an interracial administration. However, in addition to this belief (which, as far as I could determine, was genuine), there were other circumstances that dictated his course of action in this matter.

To begin with, it was always a premise of the administration that vital municipal services (police and fire protection, garbage collection, education, public health measures) had to be continued—both because the people of Gary absolutely needed them and because the failure to maintain them would represent a setback for black struggles throughout the country.

It also appeared that with a wholesale and abrupt transition to a totally new work force it would be impossible to continue these services, particularly because of a lack of the necessary skills and experiences among the black population—especially at the level of administration and skilled technical personnel. In this respect Hatcher

faced the classic problem faced by all social revolutions and
nationalist movements of recent times: after the seizure of power,
how is it possible to run a complex society when the people who
traditionally ran it are now enemies?

The strategy Hatcher employed to meet this problem was the
following. The bulk of the old personnel was retained. At the top
level of the administration (personal staff, corporation counsel, chief
of police, controller) new, trustworthy individuals were brought in.
Then, gradually, new department heads were chosen, and new rank-
and-file people included. If they had the skill already, they came at
the beginning; if they did not, they were brought in at a rate
slow enough to provide for on-the-job training from the holdovers,
without disrupting the ongoing functions of the particular department.

The main weakness of this gradualist strategy was that it permitted the old bureaucracy to survive—its institutional base was not
destroyed.

The result was that the new political priorities of the administration
could not be implemented with any degree of effectiveness in a
new municipal political practice. City government remained remarkably like what it had been in the past, at least from the
perspective of the average citizen in the community. While the
political leadership was tied up with the kinds of problems noted
earlier, the bureaucracy proceeded on its own course, which was
basically one of passive resistance. There were two aspects to this:
bureaucratic inertia, a sullen rejection of any changes in established
routine that might cause conflicts and difficulties for the employees;
and active opposition, based on politics and racism, to new methods
and goals advocated by the mayor.

To cite just one example, the mayor decided to give a very high
priority to enforcement of the housing codes, which had never
been seriously implemented by preceding administrations. After much
hard work, the Building Department was revamped to engage in
aggressive inspection work. Cases stopped being "lost," and the
number of inspections was increased by 4,000 percent, while their
quality was improved and standardized. Then it was discovered
that cases prepared for legal enforcement were being tabled by
the Legal Department on grounds of technical defects.

I personally ascertained that the alleged legal defects were
simply untrue. I then assumed that the reason for the legal staff's
behavior was that they were overburdened with work. Conferences
were held to explain to them the mayor's priorities so they could
rearrange their work schedule. Instead, a series of bitter personal

fights resulted, culminating in my removal from that area of work since the staff attorneys threatened to resign if there was continued interference with their professional responsibility. In the course of these disputes, both black and white attorneys expressed the opinion that they did not consider themselves a legal aid bureau for Gary's poor, and furthermore the root of the city's housing problem was the indolent and malicious behavior of the tenants. In their view, it was therefore unjust to vigorously enforce the existing statutes against the landlords. Thus, despite the administration's pledge, black-ghetto residents did not find their lives ameliorated in this respect.

Gradually, then, the promise of vast change after the new mayor took office came to be seen as illusory. Indeed, what actually occurred was much like an African neocolonial entity: new faces, new rhetoric and people whose lives were scarcely affected except in their feelings toward their government.

This outcome was not due to a failure of good faith on the part of the Hatcher administration. Nor does it prove the fallacious maximalist proposition that no amelioration of the people's conditions of life is possible prior to a revolution. Instead, it was due to the decline of the local mass base of the Hatcher administration and the array of national political forces confronting it.

Most black people in Gary were neither prepared nor able to take upon themselves the functions performed for them by specialized bureaucracies. They relied upon the government for education, welfare, public health, police and fire protection, enforcement of the building codes and other standards, maintenance of the public roads, and the like. Unable to develop alternative popularly based community institutions to carry on these functions by democratic self-government, the new administration was forced to rely upon the city bureaucracy—forced to pursue the option that could only result in minor changes.

Aborted Liberation

The most significant consequence of the Hatcher administration's failure to transcend the structural terrain on which it functions was political, the erosion of popular support after the successful mobilization of energies involved in the campaign. The decline of mass participation in the political process contributed in turn to the tendency of the new regime to solve its dilemmas by bureaucratic means or by relying on outside support from the federal government.

The decline in mass support ought not to be confused with a loss of votes in an election. Indeed, Hatcher is now probably secure politically as the average big-city mayor. The point is that the mass of the black population is not actively involved in helping to run the city. Thus, their political experiences are not enlarged, their understanding of the larger society and how it functions has not improved, and they are not being trained to better organize for their own interests. In short, the liberating process of the struggle for office was aborted after the initial goal was achieved—and before it could even begin to confront the profound problems faced by the mass of urban black Americans.

For example, after the inauguration, old supporters found themselves on the outside looking in. For the most part, since there was no organized effort to continue to involve them (and indeed to do so could not but conflict with the dominant strategy of the administration), they had to be content to remain passive onlookers. Moreover, the average citizen put a lot of faith in the mayor and wanted to give him an opportunity to do his job without intruding on the process.

Even among the most politicized rank-and-file elements, there was a fear of interfering. Painfully conscious of their lack of training and experience, they were afraid of "blowing it." Instead they maintained a benevolent watchfulness, an attitude reinforced by the sense that Hatcher was unique, that his performance was some kind of test of black people as a race. (Whites were not the only people encouraged by the media to think in these terms.) There were, of course, some old supporters who were frankly disillusioned: they did not receive the patronage or other assistance they had expected: they were treated rudely by a bureaucratic holdover or were merely unable to reach the ear of a leader who was once accessible as a friend.

The ebbing away of popular participation could be seen most markedly in the Spanish-speaking community, which could not reassure itself with the symbolic satisfaction of having a member of its group in the national spotlight. With even less education and prior opportunity than the blacks, they found that the qualifications barrier to municipal government left them with even less patronage than they felt to be their due reward. This feeling of betrayal was actively supported by the former machine politicians and criminal elements, who consciously evoked ethnic prejudices to isolate the mayor and weaken his popular support.

What happened in the first year of the new administration, then, was a contradiction between efficiency and ethnic solidarity. At each point the mayor felt he had to rely upon the expert bureaucracy, even at the cost of increasing his distance from his mass base. And this conflict manifested itself in a series of inexorable political events (the appointment of outside advisors, for example), each of which further contributed to eroding the popular base of the still new leadership.

As Antonio Gramsci pointed out, beneath this contradiction lies a deeper one: a historic class deprivation—inflicted on the oppressed by the very structure of the existing society—which barred the underclass from access to the skills necessary for it to run the society directly in its own interests and according to its own standard of civilization. Unless an oppressed social group is able to constitute itself as what Gramsci characterizes as a counterhegemonic social bloc, its conquest of state power cannot be much more than a change in leaders. Given the overall relation of forces in the country at large, such an undertaking was beyond the power of the black community in Gary in 1968. Therefore, dominant national-political forces were able quickly to reconstitute their overall control.

National Power

What happened to Richard Hatcher in Gary in his first year as mayor raises important questions—questions that might be of only theoretical interest if he were indeed in a unique position. He is not. [. . .] The list of black mayors will grow, and with it the question of how we are to understand the mass participation of blacks in electoral politics in this country and the future of their movement.

I believe that until new concepts are worked out, the best way of understanding this process is by analogy with certain national liberation movements in colonial or neocolonial countries. Of course, the participants—in Gary as they are in Newark—are Americans, and they are not calling for a U.N. plebiscite. But they were clearly conscious of themselves as using elections as a tool, as a step toward a much larger (though admittedly ill defined) ultimate goal— a goal whose key elements of economic change, political power, dignity, defense of a "new" culture, and so forth are very close to the ones of colonial peoples. It is because Hatcher embraced these larger objectives (without, of course, using precisely the rhetoric) that his campaign can be thought of as part of a nationalist process that has a trajectory quite similar to that of anticolonial liberation movements.

In its weakened local posture, the Hatcher administration was unable to resist successfully a large degree of cooptation by the national political authorities. [. . .] Hatcher was essentially forced to cooperate with the national government and Democratic party—even to the extent of calling on the sheriff of Cook County to send deputies to reinforce the local police when a "miniriot" occurred in the black ghetto.

Without either a nationally coordinated movement or an autonomous base of local insurgency—one capable of carrying out on a mass-scale government functions outside the official structure—Hatcher's insurgency was contained within the existing national political system. Or, to express it somewhat differently, the attempt by black forces to use the electoral process to further their national liberation was aborted by a countervailing process of neocolonialism carried out by the federal government. Bluntly speaking, the piecemeal achievement of power through parliamentary means is a fraud—at least as far as black Americans are concerned.

The process by which the national power maintained itself, and even forced the new administration to aid it in doing so, was relatively simple. As the gap between the popular constituency and the new government widened, like many another administration, Hatcher's found itself increasingly forced to rely upon its "accomplishments" to maintain its popularity and to fulfill its deeply held obligation to aid the community.

Lacking adequate autonomous financial resources—the mill remained in private hands, and it still proved impossible to assess it for tax purposes at its true value—accomplishments were necessarily dependent upon obtaining outside funds. In this case, the funds had to come from the federal government, preferably in the form of quick-performance projects to maintain popular support and to enable everyone to appear to be doing something to improve matters.

These new programs injected a flow of cash into the community, and they created many new jobs. In his first year in office, the mayor obtained in cash or pledges more federal funds than his entire local budget. Hopes began to be engendered that these programs were the key to solving local problems, while the time spent on preparing them completed the isolation of the leadership from the people.

Then, too, the stress of his forced and artificial growth created endless opportunities for nepotism and even thievery. Men who had never earned a decent living before found themselves as high-paid executives under no requirement to produce any tangible results. Indeed, federal authorities seemed glad to dispense the funds without exercising adequate controls over their expenditures. A situation arose in which people who boasted of how they were hustling the system became prisoners of its largesse.

Even the most honest and courageous leader, such as Mayor Hatcher, could not help but be trapped by the aid offered him by the federal authorities. After all, how can any elected local executive turn down millions of dollars to dispense with as he sees fit to help precisely those people he was elected to aid: The acceptance of the help guaranteed the continuation of bonds of dependence. For without any real autonomous power base, and with new vested interests and expectations created by the flow of funds into the community, and with no available alternate path of development, the relation of power between the local leader and the national state was necessarily and decisively weighted toward the latter.

In Gary, Indiana, within one year after the most prodigious feat in the history of its black population—the conquest of local political power—their insurgency had been almost totally contained. It is indeed difficult to see how the existing administration can extricate itself from its comparative impasse in the absence of fresh national developments, or of a new, more politically coherent popular upsurge from below.

There is, however, no doubt that the struggle waged by the black people of Gary, Indiana, is a landmark on their road to freedom; for the experiences of life and struggle have become another part of their heritage—and thus a promise for us all.

12

Black Rule in the Urban South?

Lee Sloan and Robert M. French

Jacksonville is a major commercial and financial city in northeast Florida, a regional center for banking and insurance. As a port city with access to the Atlantic, it serves as a major transfer point. But, like many cities, Jacksonville was caught in the familiar cycle of urban decay and suburban exodus. For Jacksonville this has meant racial transition as well. As affluent whites fled to suburban Duval County, low-income blacks crowded Jacksonville's central city. As the nonwhite population of Jacksonville approached the fifty percent mark, area whites saw a need for change. Whether racial imbalance was seen as a problem in itself or as an indicator of deeper troubles is unclear. In any case, a group of reformers proposed a solution to the city's problems—to consolidate the government of Jacksonville with that of Duval County.

City-county consolidation or "Metrogovernment" has often been proposed, but has rarely been achieved. Prior to the 1967 merger in Jacksonville-Duval, the most prominent recent instance involving major governmental reorganization was the 1962 merger of Nashville and Davidson County in Tennessee.

Individuals supporting consolidation have always presented their case in terms of "good government" reform. The reformers stress that consolidation will result in the establishment of a "rational" government that will provide increased governmental efficiency,

greater economy, expanded and improved services, greater account-
ability of public officials, the elimination of overlapping jurisdictions
and the duplication of services, the elimination of corruption, and
so forth. Further, reformers claim that consolidation facilitates the
expression of a "public interest" thus guaranteeing, as Michael
Danielson has expressed it, that "the metropolis will be governed
in the interest of the whole rather than in the conflicting interests
of its many parts."

Yet conflicting interests, and particularly racial interests, may be
crucial in determining whether or not consolidation is achieved and,
if so, its specific form. Racial transition in metropolitan areas
concentrating blacks in the central core of the city and whites
in the surrounding suburbs may lead to a point in time when
tolerance for existing governmental arrangements is drastically
reduced—a kind of political "tip point." Though the political tip
point is analogous to neighborhood or school tip points, its accompany-
ing problems are less easily resolved. Many whites cope with racial
transition in both neighborhoods and schools by simply moving out.
It may be, however, that simple evasion does not truly resolve
racial problems centered in residential neighborhoods and the
schools, but simply buys some time before the problems must be
confronted in the political realm. It is becoming increasingly evident
that whites moving out may be forfeiting political control to the
blacks who are left behind. Already black mayors have been elected
in several major cities. [. . .]

Holding the line against black power seems to be a growing
problem for metropolitan white America. Resolving it will often
involve *redefining political boundaries so that the proportion of
blacks within the new political unit is drastically decreased.* This
can assume the forms of gerrymandering or annexation, and the at-
large election is a variation of the theme. Gerrymandering is a
time-honored means of limiting or controlling such minority-group
political power. But in recent years, court decisions regarding
compliance with the one man-one vote principle have undermined
the effectiveness of the gerrymander.

Annexation, the formal addition of new territory to an existing
governmental unit, too, has provided a means of coping with the
concentration of blacks in urban centers. Though race is surely
not the only motivating force behind annexation movements, the
addition of outlying areas to the city oftentimes reduces the relative
size of the black population, for those areas annexed are often
predominantly white. The white doughnut, then, becomes a formal

part of the black center, thus reducing the relative power of the center's black citizens over their destiny. Though those whites who moved to the suburbs to escape the problems of the city will not see annexation as a panacea, the risk of forfeiting the city's government to blacks may well be sufficient to swing many white suburbanites to a proannexation position.

The at-large electoral system also may be used to limit or control black political power. In cities where blacks still constitute a numerical minority, an at-large (as opposed to a ward or district) electoral system offers assurance that the black community will either be unable to elect a black representative, or white leaders will see to it that blacks have but token conservative representation. Under an at-large system, black candidates cannot expect to win election without the financial support of white leaders and the endorsement of civic associations. Of course, if blacks become a numerical majority of the electorate, then the at-large system could work to their advantage.

Now in metropolitan areas, governmental consolidation may be emerging as a new means of dealing with the growing black threat to the existing political structure. While accomplishing the same racial goal as other techniques, it holds the promise of coping with other problems related to interdependency. Our argument should not be interpreted to imply that race is the only factor leading the residents of metropolitan areas (in Jacksonville or elsewhere) to contemplate or actually adopt a metropolitan areawide government. There are other reasons, many of which we ourselves would recognize as valid. Still we are convinced that local political elites may be deceiving themselves as well as others in failing to face the racial realities behind governmental reorganization.

Jacksonville and Duval—The Setting

At the time of consolidation, the citizens of Jacksonville and of Duval County were beset with many governmental problems, some related to governmental structure and others to governmental inaction in the past. The city charter was fifty-years old, and provided for a uniquely inefficient governmental structure. An elected five-member city commission was the major administrative body, although additional elected officials and independent boards shared administrative functions. The elected mayor, who sat on the commission, had relatively little power. Theoretically, an elected city council served as the city's legislative body. But in actuality, the commission, other elected officials, and the various independent boards all encroached upon the policymaking authority of the council. Under this complex arrangement, power and authority were so diffused that it was difficult, if not impossible, to establish governmental responsibilities.

Jacksonville's history provides a dismal record of governmental corruption. The citizens of the city have spoken for years of a machine government. Richard Martin reports that for a city of its size in 1966, Jacksonville had the largest number of full-time employees and the highest monthly payroll in the nation.

The governmental structure of Duval County provided even greater problems. The elected five-member county commission was really an administrative arm of the state government. Legislative authority rested not with the commission nor with the other sixty-nine elected county officials, but rather with the state legislature that meant, in effect, the Duval County legislative delegation. Until Florida's new constitution went into effect in 1969, local bills pertaining to Duval could be passed only during a sixty-day period every other year. Because of the tradition of "local bill courtesy" and the fact that for many years Duval County had only one state senator, that one person actually possessed veto power over all legislative matters. In brief, the county government was without the power and authority to meet the problems of an essentially urban and suburban population.

Not only were city and county governments unable to handle their own respective problems, but city-county cooperation was nearly impossible as well. As Martin points out, as many as four governmental bodies were required to have a say in any city-county project: the city council and city commission, the Duval legislative delegation, and the county commission.

Population growth was at the root of many problems in Jacksonville and Duval. Total county population doubled between 1930 and 1950, but the increase was very uneven. The growth rate in the decade of the forties, for example, was only 18.2 percent in Jacksonville but 168.4 percent in the remainder of the county. Comparable figures for the decade of the fifties were -1.7 percent and 155.6 percent. By the mid-sixties Jacksonville had an estimated population of 196,000, while the county population outside the city was estimated at 327,000.

As it is in most large metropolitan areas, a rapidly growing non-white population was centered in the core of the city. According to the 1966 Local Government Study Commission, Jacksonville ranked third in the nation in percentage of total nonwhite population for cities of over 100,000. But nonwhite population outside the city limits in Duval was only 9.2 percent of the total.

[. . .]

By the mid-sixties, both blacks and whites were aware that approximately forty-four percent of the city's population was black. *The Report of the National Advisory Commission on Civil Disorders* estimated that if current trends continued, a majority of Jacksonville's citizens would be black by 1972. Martin writes that:

> The specter of a Negro mayor and of a government dominated by Negroes became a subject of growing concern for all citizens whose thoughts ran in such directions, and there were many. In 1966 the Community Development Action Committee. . .noted tactfully that the movement of the young and higher-income groups out of the city was putting Jacksonville "under the potential control of lower-income groups who may not have a feeling of responsibility toward local government."

This racial transition was surely one of the more crucial factors leading to popular referenda to annex in both 1963 and 1964. In both instances, voters in the outlying areas voted against their being annexed.

A few black leaders in Jacksonville argued that these trends would lead inevitably to the day when black voters would outnumber whites and it would be possible to elect a black mayor and a black council. From the perspective of these persons, consolidation would lead to the dilution of the black vote just when the establishment of black political power was a distinct possibility. One black leader offered that under the old city government, all candidates for the council had to appeal to the black electorate. He argued that black voters, representing approximately forty-two percent of the total, would be foolish to support consolidation, which would reduce their share of the total electorate to approximately nineteen percent. As the most vocal black leader opposing consolidation, he charged that the black leaders supporting consolidation "sold out" the black community. This individual was generally identified as the old line, traditional Negro leader, and he had been tied to the political machine in Jacksonville for years. Other blacks believed that he opposed consolidation because the machine opposed it and because he reaped economic benefits from his promises to deliver the Negro vote, despite the widespread belief that he could no longer, in fact, deliver it.

Very few black leaders openly opposed consolidation, but the dilution argument was the basis of their opposition. These persons also argued that consolidation would not lead to governmental economy, but this was a minor theme. Several of the individuals who originally opposed consolidation were eventually neutralized or converted during the course of the consolidation movement. At any rate, only two black leaders of stature took strong positions opposing consolidation, and the other opponent was also considered to be tied to the old machine government.

Most of Jacksonville's black leaders recognized well that dilution would indeed be a consequence of consolidation, but they still found reasons to support consolidation. Foremost among those black leaders supporting consolidation was a lawyer viewed by others as moderate even though his office was noted for playing a strong role in civil-rights cases. He had made a very favorable impression on both blacks and white liberals in a losing campaign for a seat in the state legislature. Even though he probably had the best chance of becoming Jacksonville's first black mayor, he expressed his position as follows:

I argued that such a town as Jacksonville was becoming couldn't hope to attract industry or new blood. And that if that was the case, the black man obviously had more to lose than anybody else. All of the wealth in the community was outside the corporate limits. The young folks—black and white—were pretty much outside the corporate limits. All of the innovators and the creators were moving into the suburbs. That's where the industry and business was, except for a few little stores—and Main Street was declining. Main Street was a street of black faces and store windows, shop windows. The educated were in the suburbs and not in the corporate limits. Jacksonville was being run from! It would do me no good to be mayor of such a town as Jacksonville was becoming. There would certainly be no interest on the part of the people sitting out there in the suburbs if they were fighting coming in all the while.

Jacksonville's black leaders were convinced that whites were not going to allow the day to come when they would have to accept a black mayor. One embittered black leader said that whites "would have resorted to any means to prevent black control of the city." Most black leaders were convinced that the future held either consolidation or annexation, either of which would have diluted Negro voting strength. Many, though not all black leaders, were aware that the Duval legislative delegation could have annexed by merely passing a local bill, thus bypassing a popular referendum. And most were fairly certain that if consolidation failed, the delegation indeed would have passed annexation by decree.

Most black leaders, then, saw consolidation as the lesser of two evils. Recognizing that white proconsolidation leaders felt they needed to prevent a heavy negative vote in the black community, black leaders sought the best deal they could get. From the perspective of these individuals, the most important feature of the proposed charter was the provision for a council with fourteen of nineteen members elected by district. District lines were drawn to assure the election of three blacks to the council, and it was argued that blacks could also be elected to the five at-large seats. Some black leaders even felt they had promises from white leaders to support black candidates in the at-large elections. A charter requirement for regular reapportionment and compliance with the principle of one man-one vote representation also reassured black leaders.

The significance of the districting provision lies in the fact that the entire council under the old Jacksonville government had been elected at large. Nearly twenty years earlier, Jacksonville had moved from district to at-large council elections, and most observers are convinced that the rapid increase of black votes was a crucial factor in that change. It was only in the last election held under the old government that the black community succeeded in placing the first blacks on the council (in this century) [1971]. Two black women, with vastly different kinds of appeal within the black community, were elected to the council as a part of a reform government. But many black leaders were quick to observe that there was no guarantee that black candidates could continue to win at-large elections.

One might be tempted to label the districting under consolidation as benign gerrymandering since lines were drawn so as to assure representation of blacks in proportion to their county population, at least so far as district seats were concerned. White leaders who wrote the charter were of the opinion that this was a major step toward justifying the support of consolidation by black leaders. However, the authors were also aware of an ideological commitment to local representation among whites that also favored district seats on the council. Since the provision of black seats on the council may also be viewed as a concession made to assure continued white political control, however, the gerrymandering was not totally benign.

The major argument used by black leaders to support consolidation, then, stressed the assurance of black representation on the new council. These leaders discounted the election of the two Negro councilwomen under the old Jacksonville government, emphasizing that there was no guarantee that black candidates could win again at large. Parris N. Glendening and John Wesley White expressed well the rationale of those black leaders supporting consolidation: "A possibility of future Negro political power of undetermined strength was, apparently, traded for immediate power of limited strength in Duval County." From their perspective, the black community stood to gain a voice in government where it had had none in the past. This argument was strengthened by black leaders' certainty that Jacksonville and Duval County whites would not have allowed a black takeover of Jacksonville government.

Representation was not the only factor leading black leaders to support consolidation. These leaders also advanced the general argument that they had not fared well under the old governmental system. Many felt that in years past, white political leaders had maintained a machine government largely on the strength of black votes purchased cheaply at election time. One leader respected by the rank-and-file within the black community observed that consolidation would eliminate a lot of the problems blacks had lived under. "This city has suffered from political boondoggling, financial irresponsibility, and a high crime rate," he said, "and when the city suffers, the black man suffers the most."

Clean Government Campaign

Proconsolidation blacks argued that the old government was corrupt through and through, and they had plenty of evidence to back them up. Since 1965 a local TV station, through documentaries and editorials, had exposed local governmental corruption. As a result of the station's efforts a grand jury called in 1966 indicted two of five city commissioners, four of nine city councilmen, the city auditor, and the recreation chief. Charges included larceny, grand larceny, conspiracy, perjury, and the acceptance of bribes. Media reports of the trial proceedings led the public to believe that other officials avoided indictments merely because they had more cleverly covered their tracks. Thus proconsolidationists could turn the movement into a "throw the rascals out" kind of campaign, and blacks as well as whites were influenced by this appeal.

In addition to the issues of representation and governmental corruption, black proconsolidationists stressed the minor themes that the new system would yield: 1) greater employment opportunities for blacks in government, 2) tax resources from affluent suburban whites, 3) elimination of duplication of services and the overlapping of jurisdictions, 4) improved municipal services at greater economy, and 5) solutions for problems related to disaccreditation and segregation in the schools.

The arguments of the proconsolidation forces proved convincing. In August of 1967, 63.9 percent of the more than 86,000 Duval County voters who voted approved governmental consolidation. This was indeed an impressive victory. In the Nashville consolidation in 1962, only 56.8 percent of the voters favored Metro, and the reformers there had lost the first referendum in 1958. And just two months prior to the victory in Jacksonville, voters in Tampa and Hillsborough County had soundly defeated a consolidation proposal.

Aggregate voting statistics in previous consolidation referenda show Negro precincts returning heavier anticonsolidation votes than white precincts. This pattern held also in Duval, but *a healthy majority of black voters still approved consolidation.* The Jacksonville data conflict with Grubbs's study of the 1958 Nashville referendum, which concluded that "the Negroes on the whole did not favor the charter and that the higher the proportion of Negroes, the less the support for the charter." (See Table 1.)

Table 1

Anticonsolidation Vote by Race—Jacksonville

Precincts by Racial Composition	Total County Vote %
Less than 5% Negro (122)*	36.3
5-24% Negro (21)	41.6
25-49% Negro (9)	46.9
50-94% Negro (7)	43.8
95-100% Negro (28)	40.1

*Figures in parenthesis indicate the number of precincts in each category.

Source: Glendening and White 1968:3.

The difference notwithstanding, there are some striking similarities in the two successful consolidation movements in Jacksonville and Nashville. Both metropolitan areas were confronted with a rapidly growing Negro population. The threat of growing black political power, as we have seen, was a crucial factor leading Jacksonville and Duval County influentials to push for a consolidated government. Nashville whites felt similarly threatened. During the decade of the fifties, the percentage of nonwhites in the city grew from 31.4 percent to 38.1 percent. Though the first consolidation referendum was defeated in 1958, the city council passed annexation bills in 1958 and 1960 without referenda. Annexation reduced the percentage of nonwhites within the city to 27.6 percent, a figure actually lower than that in the 1940 census.

A second major similarity between Nashville and Jacksonville is that in both cities black leaders perceived themselves to be confronted with the dilemma of choosing between consolidation and annexation. We have just observed that the defeated 1958 referendum in Nashville led to hasty annexation that diluted black voting strength. In Jacksonville, two annexation referenda were voted down in the years immediately prior to the consolidation movement. But most Jacksonville black leaders were convinced that a defeat of consolidation would be followed by annexation, perhaps accomplished by the Duval legislative delegation without a referendum. Especially in Jacksonville, but also in Nashville, many black leaders reached the judgment that the probabilities of maximizing gains and minimizing losses lay in support of consolidation. It is especially interesting to note that in Nashville, the 1958 charter assured blacks of only 2 of 21 seats on the new council, but the 1962 charter assured blacks of 6 of 40 seats. In Jacksonville also, there is reason to believe that blacks were assured seats on the new council in the hope of preventing a heavy anticonsolidation vote among blacks.

A third similarity between the two cities shows the success reformers had in using consolidation as an antistatus quo movement. This strategy was employed in both cities. Apparently in Jacksonville, both black and white citizens—and perhaps especially whites in the suburbs—were influenced by the timely exposure of extensive governmental corruption. In Nashville, most observers felt that white suburbanites threw their support to Metro because they were opposed to accomplished and anticipated annexations, and because they opposed the city government's tax upon cars operated in the city by suburban residents. Nashville's Mayor Ben West provided a convenient scapegoat for the frustrations of suburban residents.

For many, a vote for Metro was a vote against the city machine and the referendum served as a purification rite.

The reform theme was missing in both the unsuccessful movements in St. Louis and Cleveland. Scott Greer concluded that, "The decision not to attack incumbent officials and existing governments for their incompetence and inability weakened the hands of the crusaders." Greer also notes that there had been some "extreme dissatisfaction" with the government of Miami, which in 1957 adopted a "federalized" form of consolidation (and thus a much weaker form of consolidation than in either Jacksonville or Nashville).

There were further dissimilarities between Jacksonville and the unsuccessful efforts to consolidate in St. Louis and Cleveland where, according to Greer, Negro wards voted almost solidly against reform. Greer cites three major reasons for black opposition to consolidation in those cities. Probably of most importance, in both St. Louis and Cleveland, blacks were fearful of losing representation in the central-city councils. A black leader in Cleveland argued that Negroes could elect two and only two representatives under the proposed system, while in Jacksonville, blacks were guaranteed greater representation under consolidation.

Greer also reported that reformers in St. Louis neglected to consult leaders from the black community. As a result black leaders made a pact *not to support anything they had had nothing to do with formulating.*

In Cleveland, black leaders were approached, but the nature of the approach, led black leaders to oppose reform. Greer quotes one black leader's sentiments:

> We have just got to stop this business of the white people treating us without any respect. Lindseth [leader of the charter campaign] came down to us, to the assembled Negro community political leaders, and he said: "Gentlemen, what is this going to cost us?"

In Jacksonville, on the other hand, white leaders supporting consolidation worked with and through black leaders in their attempt to win black proconsolidation votes. The Duval County legislative delegation saw to it that four Negroes were appointed to the study commission that was responsible for drafting the new charter. One of those four, the prominent and respected attorney discussed above (who was later to be elected at large to the new Jacksonville council), was appointed secretary of the commission and served as the major voice of the black community.

Another successful tactic used by Jacksonville reformers was to provide civil-service job protection under consolidation. Greer notes that the failure of Cleveland to make such a guarantee led to fears such as the ones expressed by one black leader:

The charter would write the protection out of civil service and you know how important civil service is to my people. They have a better shake there than in industry. They have better jobs and if you put those jobs into a county government without civil service, the chances are that a lot of people will lose their jobs.

These differences between Jacksonville's approach to reform versus that of St. Louis and Cleveland go far in explaining the differences in the extent of black support for consolidation. Blacks in Jacksonville perceived potential gains under consolidation because they had so little under the old system of government, and thus a majority of them supported consolidation. Blacks in St. Louis and Cleveland perceived potential losses under consolidation because they had something to lose, and thus they cast heavy votes against consolidation.

The history of governmental reorganization through consolidation is largely one of failure—there are few success stories. But perhaps the next few decades will change that. Since the first writing of this article [1971], Indianapolis and Marion County in Indiana were consolidated (by state legislation, bypassing a referendum).

If consolidation does become more widespread in the near future, we suspect that racial conflict will play a crucial role in the change. We would hypothesize that consolidation movements will be likely to emerge in those metropolitan areas where the proportion of blacks within the corporate limits of the city 1) is growing rapidly, and especially where it is 2) approaching forty or fifty percent.

This may well be a movement that initially will be restricted to Southern cities. In most Northern cities, a proposal of consolidation would pit the Democratic central city against the Republican suburbs. As Edward C. Banfield observed over a decade ago, "advocates of consolidation schemes are asking the Democrats to give up their control of the central cities or, at least, to place it in jeopardy." Furthermore, as Glendening and White observed, "all of the post-1945 reorganization plans for areawide government that have been accepted by the voters have been in the one-party South."

The "urge to merge" through consolidation can also be expected as a response to the election of black mayors in a number of cities and to the continuing development of Black Power with its emphasis on community control. Consolidated metropolitan government may well become a part of the backlash to the ideology and potential reality of Black Power. The major dilemma for black leaders faced with a consolidation movement becomes that stated by the black attorney in Jacksonville: to fight consolidation in the hopes of capturing the government of a dying city or to support consolidation and bring the taxes of white suburbanites back into the city. It is reported by Michael Lipsky and David J. Olson that this was also the major divisive issue in the deliberations on Newark by the Governor's Select Commission on Civil Disorders of New Jersey:

> One-half of the commissioners argued that political consolidation was the only means of establishing a tax base that would allow Newark to solve its problems. They argued that in the long run this would yield the greatest benefit to Negroes in Newark. Other commissioners argued against political consolidation on the grounds that this would, in effect, disenfranchise black people in Newark precisely at the time when their numbers had grown to constitute a majority of the city electorate. The first argument risked disturbing white suburbanites upon whom the commission felt dependent for implementation of recommendations directed at the state government. The second argument risked assuring Negroes of electoral success without the resources to provide basic services.

Newark did not consolidate, and Newark elected a black mayor. No doubt some black leaders in Jacksonville still feel that one of their own could be the mayor of their city some day soon had they fought consolidation. But most of Jacksonville's black leaders were convinced that whites would not have allowed such a development under any conditions, and they cast their lot with consolidation knowing that it destroyed any chance of their electing a black mayor—though it may have guaranteed black representation on the commission. Whether blacks should have supported consolidation or whether they got enough in return for their support are difficult judgments.

Middle-class Political Style

The rhetoric of the middle-class political style, of course, avoids the nastiness of racial conflict. A review of the public record of the consolidation movement in Jacksonville would not lead one to suspect that race was a crucial factor. Jacksonville's white elite used the good-government reform rhetoric, thus avoiding the mention of race, and still got their message of the significance of race across to individuals who were attuned. This was beautifully illustrated in the Community Development Action Committee's warning that Jacksonville could come "under the potential control of lower-income groups who may not have a feeling of responsibility toward local government." Anyone clever enough to know what "law and order" says of contemporary race relations is also clever enough to know the identity of the lower-income groups under discussion.

What happened in Jacksonville is an old story. At precisely that point in time when blacks threatened to wrest their share of political power from others, the rules of the game were changed. Black Americans may well be justified in concluding that the history of urban governmental reform reveals ever-changing attempts to conform to good government while at the same time avoiding what white Americans see as the detrimental consequences of democracy.

13

Methods Used by Blacks to Negotiate White Institutions: Mental Health Implications

Charles V. Willie

In the past, analyses of mental illness and mental health among blacks and members of other minority groups have focused on the negative consequences of life for a person in a racist society. Little attention has been given to the multitude of possible responses to racism. Fortunately, James Comer has begun to bring these alternative responses into focus. His professional experience taught him that the, "Constant daily reminders that it's tough to be black caused many youngsters enough discomfort to turn off or turn away." Then he remembered his personal experience in a family where his parents always said, "You never let race stop you from doing what you want to do." Comer concludes that the formula worked. He went to school—"hurt feelings or no hurt feelings"—got an education, and got ahead. When his self-esteem was battered, his parents patched it up and sent him back into the battle (1, p. 23). Today he is a psychiatrist and a member of the faculty at the Yale University Medical School. The professional and personal experiences of Dr. Comer illustrate that adversity can turn one off and turn one on.

Alexander Leighton also called attention to the multiple responses that individuals may make to similar situations in his study of Japanese in relocation camps in the United States. He wrote that cooperation, withdrawal, and aggressiveness are three basic

adaptations that persons may make to forces causing disturbed
emotions and thoughts; and according to the person, the circumstances,
and the interaction between the two, each form of adaptation may
free the individual from the disturbed feelings and thoughts, permit
their continuance, or lead to new pathological conditions (5, pp.
256-66).

A proper approach to the understanding of mental health in a
racist setting, then, is the investigation of how one manages adversity
successfully and unsuccessfully. According to Claudewell Thomas
and Comer, "the state of being mentally healthy represents possession
of the ability to cope or function within society in an adaptive
way"; by that they mean "the results of everyday endeavors to
cope which produce in turn a heightened capacity to cope and an
increased willingness to engage the society" (9, p. 166). Obviously,
some blacks have made successful adaptations to predominantly
white settings while others have made unsuccessful adaptations.

A brief clarification of the definition of successful adaptation
is needed. It does not refer to adjustment to and acceptance of a
racist environment in a fatalistic way. Indeed a successful response
could be the attempt to transform a racist society or transcend it
if transformation is impossible at a particular point in history. This,
of course, may result in a struggle. But René Dubos has written
that "to live is to struggle." Moreover, he states that "a successful
life is not one without ordeal, failures, and tragedies, but one during
which the person has made an adequate number of effective responses
to the constant challenge of his physical and social environment"
(2, p. 162). It was an outlook like this one that caused the distinguished
black educator Benjamin Elijah Mays, President-Emeritus of Morehouse College, to title his autobiography Born to Rebel.

Dubos calls the rebel "the standard bearer of the visionaries who
gradually increase man's ethical stature." He promised that "as
long as there are rebels in our midst, there is reason to hope that
our societies can be saved" (2, pp. 5-6). Racism is an endemic
experience at most predominantly white universities. Yet there is
reason to hope that they, too, may be saved as long as there are
rebels in their midst.

A few years ago the athletes were the rebels. Paul Hoch reports
that, "During the 1970 college football season at least seventy-nine
black athletes boycotted or were suspended from their teams over
charges of racism" (3, p. 184). At Syracuse University, probably the
most celebrated case involved eight black athletes who were
suspended from the football team because they boycotted spring

training due to the failure of the university to hire a black as a member of the nine- or ten-person coaching staff. I was a member of the Trustee-Faculty-Student Committee that investigated the charges of the black athletes. After receiving testimony from black and white football players, members of the coaching staff, and administrators of the university, our committee unanimously concluded "that racism in the Syracuse University Athletic Department is real, chronic, largely unintentional, and sustained and complicated unwittingly by many modes of behavior common in American athletics and longstanding at Syracuse University...." Then the committee branded the sanctions against the black athletes (their suspension from the football team) as a form of institutional racism unworthy of a great university because the university had not taken into consideration the racist condition of an all-white coaching staff that gave rise to the boycott. Indeed, the university had hired a black, assistant football coach following the boycott and thereby legitimized the issue raised by the black athletes. Here, then, was a racist experience at a predominantly white university to which the black students responded by withdrawing. Their method of responding resulted in effective action.

At the same university two years later, a fist fight broke out between black and white students during a Student Assembly meeting. The assembly is the legislative unit of the Syracuse University Student Association and approves the allocation of funds derived from the student-activity fee to various student groups. Up until that time, the Student Afro-American Society had no financial relationship to the Student Association largely because a few years earlier the administration of the university had made a special grant to the organizations of black students and Puerto Rican students. The black-student population had grown considerably since the time of the initial special grant. Moreover, administrative officials increasingly were of the opinion that the special financial arrangement with organizations of minority groups that enabled them to bypass direct involvement with the Student Association was paternalistic. The black students needed more funds to underwrite the costs for their expanded programs due mainly to the enlarged black population on campus. The Student Assembly initially indicated a willingness to allocate only enough funds to cover about one-fifth of the $10,000 requested by the blacks. In rejecting the request of the blacks, some Student Assembly representatives made remarks that some of the blacks felt were insulting. The fight that ensued was stimulated by these remarks. Later the Student Assembly acquiesed and allocated the Student Afro-American Society a sum of money that was about four-fifths of the initial request. The university administration made up the difference. Peace and calm returned to deliberations of the Student Assembly, which at that time had only two black members in it. Here, then, was a racist response—the failure of the Student Assembly to make adequate financial provision for the program needs of blacks—which was met by aggressiveness on the part of the oppressed. Apparently their aggressiveness was effective. The fist fight, of course, was not a necessary component of the aggressive stance. Violence is degrading to the victim and the victimizer. The aggressiveness of the black students was manifested in their massive presence at the Student Assembly in which their demands were presented, in their evening demonstration in front of a movie theater on campus, in their insistence that their demands be treated seriously, and in their rejection of the first compromise allocation as no solution.

In 1973, the student body at Syracuse University held democratic elections. The governing body for undergraduates is the Student Association, and for persons pursuing postbaccalaureate degrees, the Graduate Student Organization. Black students were elected as presidents of both of these groups for the 1973-74 academic year. They were duly elected despite the continuing presence of racism on campus. Both accepted the honor and responsibility of their high office. Here, then, was a situation in which blacks were part of the student establishment at a predominantly white university and had responsibility for maintaining the influence of the two major student-power groups on campus. One might say that these black leaders were cooperating with the system of organized student life as a way of participating in decision making on the university campus.

As indicated by Leighton, either cooperation, withdrawal, or aggressiveness may be a successful strategy or a failure, depending upon the person, the circumstances, and the interaction between these. We have described three situations, all of which were trying and difficult and each of which required different adaptations for effective participation in the university community. It is important to point out that use of one mode of adaptation in a situation that calls for another could result in failure. Despite the presence of racism in the environment as a constant experience, no single approach is always effective. Flexibility is needed.

We come now to an examination of the effect of these modes of adaptation upon the mental health of black students. Evidence from our study of black students at white colleges indicates that some black students are tending to cope with the situations with which they are confronted in a way that increases their willingness to engage the university community, while others are falling back from their encounters with whites and using a stereotyped, inflexible, and unimaginative strategy. We found the "black students moving through a series of adaptations. . .some. . .in the cooperative stage, others in the withdrawal stage, and still others in the aggressive stage" (10, p. 12). We point out that "it is well to view these stages as a series or as a continuum on which [black] students may move back and forth according to their experiences" (10, p. 13). One student with whom an interviewer had an extensive conversation had moved "from cooperation with whites to withdrawal and toward aggressiveness" because "the stress of white racism did not abate during the first and second stages of adaptation. She is tending toward aggressive radicalism now because other kinds of adaptations did not work" (10, p. 13).

It should be repeated that any form of adaptation is mentally healthy if it relieves the stress that contributes to troubled emotions and thoughts and enables the student to cope with the university community of which he or she is a part in a way that enhances both the student and the community. Thus the black football players in 1970 who withdrew, the black members of the Student Afro-American Society in 1972 who were aggressive, and the black presidents of the Student Association and the Graduate Student Organization in 1973 who led and therefore cooperated with the established student-power groups exercised adaptive methods that were situationally appropriate and effective for these students, at the specific school, during those particular times. Our research on black students and blacks in general reveals that most adapt according to the requirements of the situation and therefore survive. In *Racism and Mental Health*, the editors make this observation:

What has not been recognized by professionals and the public is the extraordinary way in which many blacks and members of other racial minorities have coped with adversity. How they have strengthened themselves to overcome the obstacles of racism is worthy of careful studies. Such investigations would make significant contributions to the accumulated body of knowledge and clinical practice in mental health. Well-documented life-styles of effectively coping individuals and families could serve as models for dealing with danger and difficulty. (11, p. 582)

A problem for black students on predominantly white, university campuses is that administrators, faculty members, and white-student colleagues often do not realize that the multitude of adaptive responses that blacks exhibit have survival value. Pathology tends to develop when blacks are encouraged or forced to ignore their existential history of racial oppression that is unlike the existential history of whites in the United States. Arthur Jensen, for example, makes this statement about precollege school-age students: "The remedy deemed logical for children who would do poorly in school is to boost their I.Q. up to where they can perform like the majority. . . ." He further states that "our diagnosis should begin. . .with the concept of the I.Q." (4, p. 3). While intellectual activity is important in elementary school, high school, and college, blacks have other concerns that are as important to survival as intellectual performance—such concerns as learning how to endure, how to develop a positive self-concept, and how to gain some control over the social environment within which one must operate. Indeed, if their adaptive activity is successful in these other areas, there is a high probability that they will also do well academically. Our study of black students at four upstate New York colleges and universities reveals that the proportion of black seniors with good grades at the A and B levels was higher than the proportion of white seniors with similar grades, although the average grade of blacks lagged behind that of whites during the first three years (10, pp. 86-87). A report on 1971 college seniors in a study conducted by the Educational Testing Service revealed that more black seniors than white seniors said they intended to earn doctorates (6, p. 16). It could be that the black seniors finally have "put it all together." Thus, the boosting of the I.Q. may not be the point at which to start for disadvantaged students as suggested by Jensen. Other concerns might take precedence for blacks.

It could be that premature focus on the intellectual performance of blacks when they should be assisted in achieving other adaptive behavior could have negative consequences, particularly in terms of self-concept. This is to say that adaptation is a function of the contemporary situational as well as the historical context of the individual and the group with which he or she is affiliated. A set of adaptive responses appropriate for one person or group in a specific setting at a particular point in time may not be appropriate for another. Thus, the adaptive responses appropriate for whites in predominantly white colleges and universities may not be appropriate for blacks in predominantly white colleges and universities.

Despite the rhetoric that calls for black separatism (which is a form of withdrawal), we found most blacks on the white college campus utilizing a range of adaptive responses (including withdrawal, cooperation, and aggressiveness) to cope with racism and other campus problems. This we consider to be mentally healthy.

Blacks do what they have to do according to the requirements of the situation. We have noticed, however, a tendency for withdrawal as an adaptive response to be used more frequently now than in the past. The black students say that they withdraw from active participation with whites as a way of avoiding insults and insensitivity. Thus, "black separatism on the predominantly white college campus cannot be understood, apart from the circumstances and conditions of life created by whites for blacks" (10, p. 13). Thus far the separatist response on the part of blacks has been a direct response to racist stimuli by whites. It is interesting to note that on the predominantly white, university campus where the undergraduate and graduate student bodies were presided over by black presidents, a proposal failed that recommended that blacks change the name of their organization from the Student Afro-American Society to the Student Association for Black Unity. Presumably, black unity is important but not of sufficient symbolic value to change the historic name of a black-campus organization in a setting where blacks are participating in the mainstream of campus student affairs as leaders. Despite this break on the tendency to move toward separatism, the tendency could accelerate if the racists' experiences persist in the campus environment. Indeed it is quite possible as we point out in *Black Students at White Colleges* that "an adaptation such as withdrawal, though originally a response to racism, may take on a life of its own and seek to perpetuate the special arrangement of a community of like-minded and lookalike people" (10, p. 13). Should this kind of adaptation become institutionalized independently from the stimuli that gave rise to it, such would constitute a pathological adjustment with the loss of freedom to change according to requirements of the situation. From what we have observed on the predominantly white, college campus, the National Advisory Commission on Civil Disorder had sufficient reason to warn that if the stress of white racism is not eliminated, soon this nation could divide permanently into two societies—one black and one white (8). This is not the campus scene at this time. But there is a lessening in the creative urge by blacks to evolve unity out of the divisions of the college community. There is more of an inclination to let each group do its own thing and to demand freedom for black self-determination without regard for what other populations on campus are doing. In some respects this inclination could further contribute to a weakened sense of community on campus and consequently less safety and security for blacks as well as whites. Such a situation, of course, would increase self-preservation anxiety for all. As the authors of the *Book of Common Prayer* would probably say, there is no health in the absence of community.

References

1. Comer, James. 1972. *Beyond Black and White*. New York: Quadrangle Books.
2. Dubos, René. 1968. *So Human an Animal*. New York: Scribner's.
3. Hoch, Paul. 1972. *Rip Off the Big Game*. Garden City, N.Y.: Doubleday.
4. Jensen, Arthur. 1969. "How Much Can We Boost I.Q. and Scholastic Achievement?" *Harvard Educational Review: Environment, Heredity, and Intelligence*. Reprint series no. 2, pp. 1-123.
5. Leighton, Alexander H. 1954. *The Governing of Man*. Princeton, N.J.: Princeton University Press.
6. Maeroff, Gene I. 1973. "Academic Goals Differ for Sexes." New York *Times*, 10 September.
7. Mays, Benjamin E. 1971. *Born to Rebel*. New York: Scribner's.
8. National Advisory Commission on Civil Disorders. 1968. *Report*. New York: Bantam.
9. Thomas, Claudewell S., and Comer, James P. 1973. "Racism and Mental Health Services." In *Racism and Mental Health*. Edited by Charles V. Willie, Bernard M. Kramer, and Bertram S. Brown. Pittsburgh, Pa.: University of Pittsburgh Press.
10. Willie, Charles V., and McCord, Arline Sakuma. 1972. *Black Students at White Colleges*. New York: Praeger.
11. Willie, Charles V.; Kramer, Bernard M.; and Brown, Bertram S. 1973. "Mental Health Action for Human Rights." In *Racism and Mental Health*. Pittsburgh, Pa.: University of Pittsburgh Press.

Epilogue

Parable of the Self-reliant Woman or the Self-righteous Man

Behold, there was an abandoned woman—young, poor, black, and beautiful. She had given birth to five children and had mothered them as best she could with with no husband in the house to help her. Neither had she parental support. The public-welfare agency would not provide for her household because the children were illegitimate and the mother would not name their fathers.

Paramours came to her house by night; they treated her as a thing. They were licentious men having a good time with no intent of staying around. They always entered under the cover of night; they always left before the break of day.

The woman wanted desperately to marry, to establish a two-parent household. Every technique she knew she tried, to fulfill the desire of every man. But none was inclined to stay. She was used and exploited sexually. She grew cynical, bitter, and lonely. No one seemed willing to help.

Her children were hungry. She loved them dearly and was determined to provide for their care. Thus she said to herself one day: "I will rely no more on anyone. I will be self-reliant. I will sell my body to save my family. I will accept no gift from any man—no money, pity, nothing!"

"I will treat each man as he deserves to be treated. I will use him as a means to an end. I will bestow my favors for pay." She was determined to be independent. She was determined to be self-reliant. She was determined to make her own way.

All men, she believed, wanted to use her. They would pay for their bloody lust. Her judgment, of course, was in error. But she had no other evidence, except her own unpleasant experience. Too often she had been exploited.

One day a good man came her way. But she could not receive his honor. She did not believe it existed. He listened to her proposition but was not interested in her mission. However, he wanted to know more about her. He wanted to know her name and how she decided on such a career.

The woman resisted but the man persisted. When the possibility of a sale seemed remote, she broke down and told her life story—how cold and cruel the world had been, how poor and hungry were her children.

He was moved to pity and was filled with compassion and wanted to help if he could. But he did not know what he could do.

The good man was an honorable citizen who cared for the poor and oppressed. He knew of his responsibility for public-welfare policy. The woman had been driven into her trade, he thought. At least, that is the way he saw it. He wanted desperately to give her money to relieve his sense of shame. What else could a good man do, he thought. What else could anyone do?

The poor woman remained adamant. No longer would she be misled. No gift would she accept from any man—no money, pity, nothing. The good man asked if he might visit her house, to see how her children were faring. With a twinkle in her eye, she invited him in, with the belief that he was not totally impossible.

He offered her money to buy food for the family. She resented and rejected his handout. She offered her body for pay and would have it no other way. She insisted her way was honorable and in the end was best for all. She was determined to be self-reliant. She was determined to provide for her own.

What else could a good man do, he thought. What else could anyone do? How could a good man help her? So, he lay with her that night. She would have it no other way. No gift would she accept from any man. No money, pity, nothing. She offered her body for pay.

He was irritable, uncomfortable, and agitated. Into his midsection he plunged a penknife. That night he died in her bed. He also left before sunrise. He also left before the break of day. Her feeling of despair was almost unbearable. Was it because of his "virtue" or was it because of her "vice"?

Contributors

W. Curtis Banks—"Attribution of Prejudice to Self and Others"—is assistant professor of psychology at Princeton University.

Fred Barbaro—"Ethnic Resentment"—is the Assistant Dean for Academic Affairs and associate professor in the School of Social Work at Adelphi University.

Nijole V. Benokraitis—"Institutional Racism: A Perspective in Search of Clarity and Research"—is professor of sociology at the University of Baltimore, Maryland.

Ann H. Beuf—"Racial Attitudes of Native-American Preschoolers" —is assistant professor of sociology at the University of Pennsylvania.

Joe R. Feagin—"Institutional Racism: A Perspective in Search of Clarity and Research"—is professor of sociology at the University of Texas at Austin.

Robert M. French—"Black Rule in the Urban South?"—was formerly with the Department of Sociology of Florida State University at Tallahassee.

Jewelle Taylor Gibbs—"Black Students at Integrated Colleges: Problems and Prospects"—is doing postdoctoral studies in clinical psychology at the University of California at Berkeley.

Edward Greer—"The 'Liberation' of Gary, Indiana"—was the former director of the Urban Affairs Program at Wheaton College.

Janet L. Hubbard—"Attribution of Prejudice to Self and Others"—is with the Department of Psychology at the University of California at Los Angeles.

Linda J. M. LaRue—"Black Liberation and Women's Lib"—was formerly with the Department of Government at Cornell University.

David Owens—"A Vision of Despair by an Angry Black Writer: John Williams and *The Man Who Cried I Am*"—is professor of English at Syracuse University.

Lee Sloan—"Black Rule in the Urban South?"—is senior research associate at the Center for Policy Research in New York City.

Joseph S. Vannoy—"Attribution of Prejudice to Self and Others"—is associate professor in the Department of Psychology at Miami University, Ohio.

Meyer Weinberg—"A Historical Framework for Multicultural Education"—is director of the Center for Equal Education in the School of Education at Northwestern University and editor of *Integrated Education.*

Charles V. Willie—"A National Population Policy and the Fear of Racial Genocide," "Community Development and Social Change," "Methods Used by Blacks to Negotiate White Institutions: Mental Health Implications," and editor—is professor of education and urban studies at the Graduate School of Education at Harvard University.

Index

Soc
E
184
A 1
B 553